D0909237

ELIZABETH BARRETT BROWNING

VOLUME V.

AMS PRESS
NEW YORK

Elizabeth Barrett Browning
Rome - February 1859

Aurora Leigh
a poem in nine books
Book V to Book IX

THOMAS·Y·CROWELL·&
COMPANY·NEW~YORK

THE COMPLETE WORKS

OF

ELIZABETH BARRETT BROWNING

Edited with Introductions and Notes by

CHARLOTTE PORTER AND HELEN A. CLARKE

Editors of Robert Browning's Works, Camberwell
Edition; Authors of " Browning Study
Programmes," etc.

VOLUME V.

NEW YORK
THOMAS Y. CROWELL & CO.
PUBLISHERS

1900

Library of Congress Cataloging in Publication Data

Browning, Elizabeth (Barrett) 1806-1861.
 The complete works of Elizabeth Barrett Browning.

 Reprint of the 1900 ed.
 CONTENTS: v. 1. Biographical introduction.
Critical introduction. Chronological bibliography.
Battle of the Marathon. Essay on mind. Juvenilia.
Seraphim, and other poems.--v. 2. Romaunt of Margret.
Drama of exile. Lady Geraldine. Vision of poets, and
other poems.--v. 3. Duchess May. Sonnets from the
Portugese. Case Guidi windows. Poems before congress.
--[Etc.]
 I. Porter, Charlotte Endymion, 1859-1942, ed.
II. Clarke, Helen Archibald, d. 1926, ed.

PR4180.F73   821'.8   74-148759
ISBN 0-404-08840-6

Reprinted from the edition of 1900, New York
First AMS edition published in 1973
Manufactured in the United States of America

International Standard Book Number:
Complete Set: 0-404-08840-6
Volume 5: 0-404-08845-7

AMS PRESS INC.
NEW YORK, N. Y.   10003

CONTENTS.

AURORA LEIGH.

1856.

FIFTH BOOK.

AURORA LEIGH, be humble.   Shall I hope
To speak my poems in mysterious tune
With man and nature ? — with the lava-lymph
That trickles from successive galaxies
Still drop by drop adown the finger of God
In still new worlds ? — with summer-days in this
That scarce dare breathe they are so beautiful ?
With spring's delicious trouble in the ground,
Tormented by the quickened blood of roots,
And softly pricked by golden crocus-sheaves   10
In token of the harvest-time of flowers ?
With winters and with autumns, — and beyond
With the human heart's large seasons, when it hopes
And fears, joys, grieves, and loves ? — with all that strain
Of sexual passion, which devours the flesh
In a sacrament of souls ? with mother's breasts
Which, round the new-made creatures hanging there,
Throb luminous and harmonious like pure spheres ? —
With multitudinous life, and finally
With the great escapings of ecstatic souls,   20
Who, in a rush of too long prisoned flame,
Their radiant faces upward, burn away
This dark of the body, issuing on a world
Beyond our mortal ? — can I speak my verse
So plainly in tune to these things and the rest

That men shall feel it catch them on the quick
As having the same warrant over them
To hold and move them if they will or no,
Alike imperious as the primal rhythm
Of that theurgic nature ? — I must fail,　　　　30
Who fail at the beginning to hold and move
One man, — and he my cousin, and he my friend,
And he born tender, made intelligent,
Inclined to ponder the precipitous sides
Of difficult questions ; yet, obtuse to *me*,
Of *me*, incurious ! likes me very well,
And wishes me a paradise of good,
Good looks, good means, and good digestion, — ay,
But otherwise evades me, puts me off
With kindness, with a tolerant gentleness, —　　40
Too light a book for a grave man's reading !　Go,
Aurora Leigh : be humble.
　　　　　　　　　　There it is,
We women are too apt to look to one,
Which proves a certain impotence in art.
We strain our natures at doing something great,
Far less because it's something great to do,
Than haply that we, so, commend ourselves
As being not small, and more appreciable
To some one friend.　We must have mediators
Betwixt our highest conscience and the judge ;　　50
Some sweet saint's blood must quicken in our palms,
Or all the like in heaven seems slow and cold :
Good only being perceived as the end of good,
And God alone pleased, — that's too poor, we think,
And not enough for us by any means.
Ay — Romney, I remember, told me once
We miss the abstract when we comprehend.
We miss it most when we aspire, — and fail.

Yet, so, I will not. — This vile woman's way
Of trailing garments shall not trip me up :   60
I'll have no traffic with the personal thought
In Art's pure temple.   Must I work in vain,
Without the approbation of a man ?
It cannot be ; it shall not.   Fame itself,
That approbation of the general race,
Presents a poor end (though the arrow speed
Shot straight with vigorous finger to the white),
And the highest fame was never reached except
By what was aimed above it.   Art for art,
And good for God Himself, the essential Good !   70
We'll keep our aims sublime, our eyes erect,
Although our woman-hands should shake and fail ;
And if we fail . . . But must we ? —

                    Shall I fail ?
The Greeks said grandly in their tragic phrase,
" Let no one be called happy till his death."
To which I add, — Let no one till his death
Be called unhappy.   Measure not the work
Until the day's out and the labour done,
Then bring your gauges.   If the day's work's scant,
Why, call it scant ; affect no compromise ;   80
And, in that we have nobly striven at least,
Deal with us nobly, women though we be,
And honour us with truth if not with praise.

My ballads prospered ; but the ballad's race
Is rapid for a poet who bears weights
Of thought and golden image.   He can stand
Like Atlas, in the sonnet, — and support
His own heavens pregnant with dynastic stars ;
But then he must stand still, nor take a step.

In that descriptive poem called " The Hills,"   90
The prospects were too far and indistinct.
'Tis true my critics said " A fine view, that ! "
The public scarcely cared to climb my book
For even the finest, and the public's right ;
A tree's mere firewood, unless humanised, —
Which well the Greeks knew when they stirred its bark
With close-pressed bosoms of subsiding nymphs,
And made the forest-rivers garrulous
With babble of gods.   For us, we are called to mark
A still more intimate humanity   100
In this inferior nature, or ourselves
Must fall like dead leaves trodden underfoot
By veritable artists.   Earth (shut up
By Adam, like a fakir in a box
Left too long buried) remained stiff and dry,
A mere dumb corpse, till Christ the Lord came down,
Unlocked the doors, forced open the blank eyes,
And used His kingly chrism to straighten out
The leathery tongue turned back into the throat ;
Since when, she lives, remembers, palpitates   110
In every limb, aspires in every breath,
Embraces infinite relations.   Now
We want no half-gods, Panomphæan Joves,
Fauns, Naiads, Tritons, Oreads and the rest,
To take possession of a senseless world
To unnatural vampire-uses.   See the earth,
The body of our body, the green earth,
Indubitably human like this flesh
And these articulated veins through which
Our heart drives blood.   There's not a flower of
      spring   120
That dies ere June but vaunts itself allied
By issue and symbol, by significance

And correspondence, to that spirit-world
Outside the limits of our space and time,
Whereto we are bound.   Let poets give it voice
With human meanings, — else they miss the thought,
And henceforth step down lower, stand confessed
Instructed poorly for interpreters,
Thrown out by an easy cowslip in the text.
Even so my pastoral failed : it was a book   130
Of surface-pictures — pretty, cold, and false
With literal transcript, — the worse done, I think,
For being not ill-done : let me set my mark
Against such doings, and do otherwise.
This strikes me. — If the public whom we know
Could catch me at such admissions, I should pass
For being right modest.   Yet how proud we are,
In daring to look down upon ourselves !

The critics say that epics have died out
With Agamemnon and the goat-nursed gods ;   140
I'll not believe it.   I could never deem,
As Payne Knight did (the mythic mountaineer
Who travelled higher than he was born to live,
And showed sometimes the goitre in his throat
Discoursing of an image seen through fog),
That Homer's heroes measured twelve feet high.
They were but men : — his Helen's hair turned grey
Like any plain Miss Smith's who wears a front ;
And Hector's infant whimpered at a plume
As yours last Friday at a turkey-cock.   150
All actual heroes are essential men,
And all men possible heroes : every age,
Heroic in proportions, double-faced,
Looks backward and before, expects a morn
And claims an epos.

                                        Ay, but every age
Appears to souls who live in't (ask Carlyle)
Most unheroic.   Ours, for instance, ours :
The thinkers scout it, and the poets abound
Who scorn to touch it with a finger-tip :
A pewter age, — mixed metal, silver-washed ;   160
An age of scum, spooned off the richer past,
An age of patches for old gaberdines,
An age of mere transition, meaning nought
Except that what succeeds must shame it quite
If God please.   That's wrong thinking, to my mind,
And wrong thoughts make poor poems.
                                        Every age,
Through being beheld too close, is ill-discerned
By those who have not lived past it.   We'll suppose
Mount Athos carved, as Alexander schemed,
To some colossal statue of a man.   170
The peasants, gathering brushwood in his ear,
Had guessed as little as the browsing goats
Of form or feature of humanity
Up there, — in fact, had travelled five miles off
Or ere the giant image broke on them,
Full human profile, nose and chin distinct,
Mouth, muttering rhythms of silence up the sky
And fed at evening with the blood of suns ;
Grand torso, — hand, that flung perpetually
The largesse of a silver river down   180
To all the country pastures.   'Tis even thus
With times we live in, — evermore too great
To be apprehended near.
                                But poets should
Exert a double vision ; should have eyes
To see near things as comprehensively
As if afar they took their point of sight,

And distant things as intimately deep
As if they touched them.   Let us strive for this.
I do distrust the poet who discerns
No character or glory in his times,   190
And trundles back his soul five hundred years,
Past moat and drawbridge, into a castle-court,
To sing — oh, not of lizard or of toad
Alive i' the ditch there, — 'twere excusable,
But of some black chief, half knight, half sheep-lifter,
Some beauteous dame, half chattel and half queen,
As dead as must be, for the greater part,
The poems made on their chivalric bones ;
And that's no wonder : death inherits death.

Nay, if there's room for poets in this world   200
A little overgrown (I think there is),
Their sole work is to represent the age,
Their age, not Charlemagne's, — this live, throbbing
        age,
That brawls, cheats, maddens, calculates, aspires,
And spends more passion, more heroic heat,
Betwixt the mirrors of its drawing-rooms,
Than Roland with his knights at Roncesvalles.
To flinch from modern varnish, coat or flounce,
Cry out for togas and the picturesque,
Is fatal, — foolish too.   King Arthur's self   210
Was commonplace to Lady Guenever ;
And Camelot to minstrels seemed as flat
As Fleet Street to our poets.
                            Never flinch,
But still, unscrupulously epic, catch
Upon the burning lava of a song
The full-veined, heaving, double-breasted Age :
That, when the next shall come, the men of that

May touch the impress with reverent hand, and say
" Behold, — behold the paps we all have sucked !
This bosom seems to beat still, or at least   220
It sets ours beating : this is living art,
Which thus presents and thus records true life."

What form is best for poems ?   Let me think
Of forms less, and the external.   Trust the spirit,
As sovran nature does, to make the form ;
For otherwise we only imprison spirit
And not embody.   Inward evermore
To outward, — so in life, and so in art
Which still is life.
                    Five acts to make a play.
And why not fifteen ? why not ten ? or seven ?   230
What matter for the number of the leaves,
Supposing the tree lives and grows ? exact
The literal unities of time and place,
When 'tis the essence of passion to ignore
Both time and place ?   Absurd.   Keep up the fire,
And leave the generous flames to shape themselves.

'Tis true the stage requires obsequiousness
To this or that convention ; " exit " here
And " enter " there ; the points for clapping, fixed,
Like Jacob's white-peeled rods before the rams,   240
And all the close-curled imagery clipped
In manner of their fleece at shearing time.
Forget to prick the galleries to the heart
Precisely at the fourth act, — culminate
Our five pyramidal acts with one act more,
We're lost so : Shakespeare's ghost could scarcely plead
Against our just damnation.   Stand aside ;
We'll muse for comfort that, last century,

On this same tragic stage on which we have failed,
A wigless Hamlet would have failed the same.   250

And whosoever writes good poetry,
Looks just to art.   He does not write for you
Or me, — for London or for Edinburgh ;
He will not suffer the best critic known
To step into his sunshine of free thought
And self-absorbed conception and exact
An inch-long swerving of the holy lines.
If virtue done for popularity
Defiles like vice, can art, for praise or hire,
Still keep its splendour and remain pure art ?   260
Eschew such serfdom.   What the poet writes,
He writes : mankind accepts it if it suits,
And that's success : if not, the poem's passed
From hand to hand, and yet from hand to hand
Until the unborn snatch it, crying out
In pity on their fathers' being so dull,
And that's success too.

               I will write no plays ;
Because the drama, less sublime in this,
Makes lower appeals, submits more menially,
Adopts the standard of the public taste   270
To chalk its height on, wears a dog-chain round
Its regal neck, and learns to carry and fetch
The fashions of the day to please the day,
Fawns close on pit and boxes, who clap hands
Commending chiefly its docility
And humour in stage-tricks, — or else indeed
Gets hissed at, howled at, stamped at like a dog,
Or worse, we'll say.   For dogs, unjustly kicked,
Yell, bite at need ; but if your dramatist
(Being wronged by some five hundred nobodies   280

Because their grosser brains most naturally
Misjudge the fineness of his subtle wit)
Shows teeth an almond's breadth, protests the length
Of a modest phrase, — "My gentle countrymen,
" There's something in it haply of your fault," —
Why then, besides five hundred nobodies,
He'll have five thousand and five thousand more
Against him, — the whole public, — all the hoofs
Of King Saul's father's asses, in full drove,
And obviously deserve it.   He appealed   290
To these, — and why say more if they condemn,
Than if they praise him ? — Weep, my Æschylus,
But low and far, upon Sicilian shores !
For since 'twas Athens (so I read the myth)
Who gave commission to that fatal weight
The tortoise, cold and hard, to drop on thee
And crush thee, — better cover thy bald head ;
She'll hear the softest hum of Hyblan bee
Before thy loudest protestation !
                                        Then
The risk's still worse upon the modern stage.   300
I could not, for so little, accept success,
Nor would I risk so much, in ease and calm,
For manifester gains : let those who prize,
Pursue them : I stand off.   And yet, forbid
That any irreverent fancy or conceit
Should litter in the Drama's throne-room where
The rulers of our art, in whose full veins
Dynastic glories mingle, sit in strength
And do their kingly work, — conceive, command,
And, from the imagination's crucial heat,   310
Catch up their men and women all a-flame
For action, all alive and forced to prove
Their life by living out heart, brain, and nerve,

Until mankind makes witness, " These be men
As we are," and vouchsafes the greeting due
To Imogen and Juliet — sweetest kin
On art's side.

            'Tis that, honouring to its worth
The drama, I would fear to keep it down
To the level of the footlights.   Dies no more
The sacrificial goat, for Bacchus slain,   320
His filmed eyes fluttered by the whirling white
Of choral vestures, — troubled in his blood,
While tragic voices that clanged keen as swords,
Leapt high together with the altar-flame
And made the blue air wink.   The waxen mask,
Which set the grand still front of Themis' son
Upon the puckered visage of a player, —
The buskin, which he rose upon and moved,
As some tall ship first conscious of the wind   329
Sweeps slowly past the piers, — the mouthpiece, where
The mere man's voice with all its breaths and breaks
Went sheathed in brass, and clashed on even heights
Its phrasèd thunders, — these things are no more,
Which once were.   And concluding, which is clear,
The growing drama has outgrown such toys
Of simulated stature, face, and speech,
It also peradventure may outgrow
The simulation of the painted scene,
Boards, actors, prompters, gaslight, and costume,
And take for a worthier stage the soul itself,   340
Its shifting fancies and celestial lights,
With all its grand orchestral silences
To keep the pauses of its rhythmic sounds.

Alas, I still see something to be done,
And what I do falls short of what I see,

Though I waste myself on doing.   Long green days,
Worn bare of grass and sunshine, — long calm nights
From which the silken sleeps were fretted out,
Be witness for me, with no amateur's
Irreverent haste and busy idleness   350
I set myself to art !   What then ? what's done ?
What's done, at last ?

                 Behold, at last, a book.
If life-blood's necessary, which it is, —
(By that blue vein athrob on Mahomet's brow,
Each prophet-poet's book must show man's blood !)
If life-blood's fertilising, I wrung mine
On every leaf of this, — unless the drops
Slid heavily on one side and left it dry.
That chances often : many a fervid man
Writes books as cold and flat as graveyard stones 360
From which the lichen's scraped ; and if Saint Preux
Had written his own letters, as he might,
We had never wept to think of the little mole
'Neath Julie's drooping eyelid.   Passion is
But something suffered, after all.

                     While Art
Sets action on the top of suffering :
The artist's part is both to be and do,
Transfixing with a special, central power
The flat experience of the common man,
And turning outward, with a sudden wrench,   370
Half agony, half ecstasy, the thing
He feels the inmost, — never felt the less
Because he sings it.   Does a torch less burn
For burning next reflectors of blue steel,
That *he* should be the colder for his place
'Twixt two incessant fires, — his personal life's
And that intense refraction which burns back

Perpetually against him from the round
Of crystal conscience he was born into
If artist-born ?   O sorrowful great gift   380
Conferred on poets, of a twofold life,
When one life has been fond enough for pain !
We, staggering 'neath our burden as mere men,
Being called to stand up straight as demigods,
Support the intolerable strain and stress
Of the universal, and send clearly up,
With voices broken by the human sob,
Our poems to find rhymes among the stars !
But soft,— a " poet " is a word soon said,
A book's a thing soon written.   Nay, indeed,   390
The more the poet shall be questionable,
The more unquestionably comes his book.
And this of mine — well, granting to myself
Some passion in it, — furrowing up the flats,
Mere passion will not prove a volume worth
Its gall and rags even.   Bubbles round a keel
Mean nought, excepting that the vessel moves.
There's more than passion goes to make a man
Or book, which is a man too.
                     I am sad.
I wonder if Pygmalion had these doubts   400
And, feeling the hard marble first relent,
Grow supple to the straining of his arms,
And tingle through its cold to his burning lip,
Supposed his senses mocked, supposed the toil
Of stretching past the known and seen to reach
The archetypal Beauty out of sight,
Had made his heart beat fast enough for two,
And with his own life dazed and blinded him !
Not so ; Pygmalion loved,— and whoso loves
Believes the impossible.

But I am sad :   410
I cannot thoroughly love a work of mine,
Since none seems worthy of my thought and hope
More highly mated.   He has shot them down,
My Phœbus Apollo, soul within my soul,
Who judges, by the attempted, what's attained,
And with the silver arrow from his height
Has struck down all my works before my face
While I said nothing.   Is there aught to say ?
I called the artist but a greatened man.
He may be childless also, like a man.   420

I laboured on alone.   The wind and dust
And sun of the world beat blistering in my face ;
And hope, now for me, now against me, dragged
My spirits onward, as some fallen balloon,
Which, whether caught by blossoming tree or bare,
Is torn alike.   I sometimes touched my aim,
Or seemed,— and generous souls cried out " Be
        strong,
Take courage ; now you're on our level,— now !
The next step saves you ! "   I was flushed with
        praise,
But, pausing just a moment to draw breath,   430
I could not choose but murmur to myself
" Is this all ? all that's done ? and all that's gained ?
If this then be success, 'tis dismaller
Than any failure."
                        O my God, my God,
O supreme Artist, who as sole return
For all the cosmic wonder of Thy work,
Demandest of us just a word . . . a name,
" My Father ! " thou hast knowledge, only thou,
How dreary 'tis for women to sit still,

On winter nights by solitary fires, 440
And hear the nations praising them far off,
Too far! ay, praising our quick sense of love,
Our very heart of passionate womanhood,
Which could not beat so in the verse without
Being present also in the unkissed lips
And eyes undried because there's none to ask
The reason they grew moist.
          To sit alone
And think for comfort how, that very night,
Affianced lovers, leaning face to face
With sweet half-listenings for each other's breath, 450
Are reading haply from a page of ours,
To pause with a thrill (as if their cheeks had touched)
When such a stanza, level to their mood,
Seems floating their own thought out — "So I feel
For thee," — "And I, for thee : this poet knows
What everlasting love is!" — how, that night,
Some father, issuing from the misty roads
Upon the luminous round of lamp and hearth
And happy children, having caught up first
The youngest there until it shrink and shriek 460
To feel the cold chin prick its dimples through
With winter from the hills, may throw i' the lap
Of the eldest (who has learnt to drop her lids
To hide some sweetness newer than last year's)
Our book and cry, . . . "Ah you, you care for
      rhymes ;
So here be rhymes to pore on under trees,
When April comes to let you! I've been told
They are not idle as so many are,
But set hearts beating pure as well as fast.
'Tis yours, the book ; I'll write your name in it, 470
That so you may not lose, however lost

In poet's lore and charming reverie,
The thought of how your father thought of *you*
In riding from the town."
                              To have our books
Appraised by love, associated with love,
While *we* sit loveless ! is it hard, you think ?
At least 'tis mournful.   Fame, indeed, 'twas said,
Means simply love.   It was a man said that :
And then, there's love and love : the love of all
(To risk in turn a woman's paradox)   480
Is but a small thing to the love of one.
You bid a hungry child be satisfied
With a heritage of many corn-fields : nay,
He says he's hungry,— he would rather have
That little barley-cake you keep from him
While reckoning up his harvests.   So with us
(Here, Romney, too, we fail to generalise) :
We're hungry.
                        Hungry ! but it's pitiful
To wail like unweaned babes and suck our thumbs
Because we're hungry.   Who, in all this world   490
(Wherein we are haply set to pray and fast
And learn what good is by its opposite),
Has never hungered ?   Woe to him who has found
The meal enough ! if Ugolino's full,
His teeth have crunched some foul unnatural thing,
For here satiety proves penury
More utterly irremediable.   And since
We needs must hunger,— better, for man's love,
Than God's truth ! better, for companions sweet,
Than great convictions ! let us bear our weights,   500
Preferring dreary hearths to desert souls.
Well, well ! they say we're envious, we who rhyme ;
But I, because I am a woman perhaps

And so rhyme ill, am ill at envying.
I never envied Graham his breadth of style,
Which gives you, with a random smutch or two
(Near sighted critics analyse to smutch),
Such delicate perspectives of full life :
Nor Belmore, for the unity of aim
To which he cuts his cedarn poems, fine   510
As sketchers do their pencils : nor Mark Gage,
For that caressing colour and trancing tone
Whereby you're swept away and melted in
The sensual element, which with a back wave
Restores you to the level of pure souls
And leaves you with Plotinus.   None of these,
For native gifts or popular applause,
I've envied ; but for this,— that when by chance
Says some one,— "There goes Belmore, a great
      man !
He leaves clean work behind him, and requires   520
No sweeper up of the chips," . . . a girl I know,
Who answers nothing, save with her brown eyes,
Smiles unaware as if a guardian saint
Smiled in her : — for this, too,— that Gage comes
      home
And lays his last book's prodigal review
Upon his mother's knee, where, years ago,
He laid his childish spelling-book and learned
To chirp and peck the letters from her mouth,
As young birds must.   "Well done," she murmured
      then;
She will not say it now more wonderingly :   530
And yet the last "Well done" will touch him
      more,
As catching up to-day and yesterday
In a perfect chord of love : and so, Mark Gage,

I envy you your mother ! — and you, Graham,
Because you have a wife who loves you so,
She half forgets, at moments, to be proud
Of being Graham's wife, until a friend observes,
"The boy here has his father's massive brow
Done small in wax . . . if we push back the curls."
Who loves me ?   Dearest father, — mother sweet,—
I speak the names out sometimes by myself,   541
And make the silence shiver.   They sound strange,
As Hindostanee to an Ind-born man
Accustomed many years to English speech ;
Or lovely poet-words grown obsolete,
Which will not leave off singing.   Up in heaven
I have my father, — with my mother's face
Beside him in a blotch of heavenly light ;
No more for earth's familiar, household use,
No more.   The best verse written by this hand   550
Can never reach them where they sit, to seem
Well done to *them*.   Death quite unfellows us,
Sets dreadful odds betwixt the live and dead,
And makes us part as those at Babel did
Through sudden ignorance of a common tongue.
A living Cæsar would not dare to play
At bowls with such as my dead father is.

And yet this may be less so than appears,
This change and separation.   Sparrows five
For just two farthings, and God cares for each.   560
If God is not too great for little cares,
Is any creature, because gone to God ?
I've seen some men, veracious, nowise mad,
Who have thought or dreamed, declared and testified
They heard the Dead a-ticking like a clock
Which strikes the hours of the eternities,

Beside them, with their natural ears, — and known
That human spirits feel the human way
And hate the unreasoning awe which waves them off
From possible communion.   It may be.   570
At least, earth separates as well as heaven.
For instance, I have not seen Romney Leigh
Full eighteen months . . . add six, you get two
        years.
They say he's very busy with good works, —
Has parted Leigh Hall into almshouses.
He made one day an almshouse of his heart,
Which ever since is loose upon the latch
For those who pull the string. — I never did.

It always makes me sad to go abroad,
And now I'm sadder that I went to-night,   580
Among the lights and talkers at Lord Howe's.
His wife is gracious, with her glossy braids,
And even voice, and gorgeous eyeballs, calm
As her other jewels.   If she's somewhat cold,
Who wonders, when her blood has stood so long
In the ducal reservoir she calls her line
By no means arrogantly ? she's not proud ;
Not prouder than the swan is of the lake
He has always swum in ; — 'tis her element ;
And so she takes it with a natural grace,   590
Ignoring tadpoles.   She just knows perhaps
There *are* who travel without outriders,
Which isn't her fault.   Ah, to watch her face,
When good Lord Howe expounds his theories
Of social justice and equality !
'Tis curious, what a tender, tolerant bend
Her neck takes : for she loves him, likes his talk,
" Such clever talk — that dear, odd Algernon ! "

She listens on, exactly as if he talked
Some Scandinavian myth of Lemures,   600
Too pretty to dispute, and too absurd.
She's gracious to me as her husband's friend,
And would be gracious were I not a Leigh,
Being used to smile just so, without her eyes,
On Joseph Strangways the Leeds mesmerist,
And Delia Dobbs the lecturer from "the States"
Upon the "Woman's question."   Then, for him,
I like him ; he's my friend.   And all the rooms
Were full of crinkling silks that swept about
The fine dust of most subtle courtesies.   610
What then ? — why then, we come home to be sad.

How lovely, One I love not looked to-night !
She's very pretty, Lady Waldemar.
Her maid must use both hands to twist that coil
Of tresses, then be careful lest the rich
Bronze rounds should slip : — she missed, though, a
          grey hair,
A single one, — I saw it ; otherwise
The woman looked immortal.   How they told,
Those alabaster shoulders and bare breasts,   619
On which the pearls, drowned out of sight in milk,
Were lost, excepting for the ruby clasp !
They split the amaranth velvet-bodice down
To the waist or nearly, with the audacious press
Of full-breathed beauty.   If the heart within
Were half as white ! — but, if it were, perhaps
The breast were closer covered and the sight
Less aspectable by half, too.
                    I heard
The young man with the German student's look —
A sharp face, like a knife in a cleft stick,

Which shot up straight against the parting line   630
So equally dividing the long hair, —
Say softly to his neighbor (thirty-five
And mediæval), " Look that way, Sir Blaise.
She's Lady Waldemar — to the left — in red —
Whom Romney Leigh, our ablest man just now,
Is soon about to marry."
                    Then replied
Sir Blaise Delorme, with quiet, priestlike voice,
Too used to syllable damnations round
To make a natural emphasis worth while :
" Is Leigh your ablest man ? the same, I think,   640
Once jilted by a recreant pretty maid
Adopted from the people ?   Now, in change,
He seems to have plucked a flower from the other side
Of the social hedge."
                " A flower, a flower," exclaimed
My German student, — his own eyes full-blown
Bent on her.   He was twenty, certainly.

Sir Blaise resumed with gentle arrogance,
As if he had dropped his alms into a hat
And gained the right to counsel, — " My young friend,
I doubt your ablest man's ability   650
To get the least good or help meet for him,
For pagan phalanstery or Christian home,
From such a flowery creature."
                        " Beautiful !"
My student murmured rapt, — " Mark how she stirs !
Just waves her head, as if a flower indeed,
Touched far off by the vain breath of our talk."

At which that bilious Grimwald (he who writes
For the Renovator), who had seemed absorbed
Upon the table-book of autographs
(I dare say mentally he crunched the bones　　660
Of all those writers, wishing them alive
To feel his tooth in earnest), turned short round
With low carnivorous laugh, — " A flower, of
　　course !
She neither sews nor spins, — and takes no thought
Of her garments . . . falling off."
　　　　　　　　　　The student flinched ;
Sir Blaise, the same ; then both, drawing back their
　　chairs
As if they spied black-beetles on the floor,
Pursued their talk, without a word being thrown
To the critic.
　　　　　　Good Sir Blaise's brow is high
And noticeably narrow : a strong wind,　　670
You fancy, might unroof him suddenly,
And blow that great top attic off his head
So piled with feudal relics.　You admire
His nose in profile, though you miss his chin ;
But, though you miss his chin, you seldom miss
His ebon cross worn innermostly (carved
For penance by a saintly Styrian monk
Whose flesh was too much with him), slipping
　　through
Some unaware unbuttoned casualty
Of the under-waistcoat.　With an absent air　　680
Sir Blaise sat fingering it and speaking low,
While I, upon the sofa, heard it all.

" My dear young friend, if we could bear our eyes,
Like blessedest Saint Lucy, on a plate,

They would not trick us into choosing wives,
As doublets, by the colour.   Otherwise
Our fathers chose, — and therefore, when they had
    hung
Their household keys about a lady's waist,
The sense of duty gave her dignity ;
She kept her bosom holy to her babes,   690
And, if a moralist reproved her dress,
'Twas 'Too much starch !' — and not 'Too little
    lawn !' ''

" Now, pshaw ! " returned the other in a heat,
A little fretted by being called " young friend,"
Or so I took it, — " for Saint Lucy's sake,
If she's the saint to swear by, let us leave
Our fathers, — plagued enough about our sons ! "
(He stroked his beardless chin) " yes, plagued, sir,
    plagued :
The future generations lie on us
As heavy as the nightmare of a seer ;   700
Our meat and drink grow painful prophecy :
I ask you, — have we leisure, if we liked,
To hollow out our weary hands to keep
Your intermittent rushlight of the past
From draughts in lobbies?   Prejudice of sex
And marriage-law . . . the socket drops them
    through
While we two speak, — however may protest
Some over-delicate nostrils like your own,
'Gainst odours thence arising."

                      " You are young,"
Sir Blaise objected.

              " If I am," he said   710
With fire, — " though somewhat less so than I seem,

The young run on before, and see the thing
That's coming.   Reverence for the young, I cry.
In that new church for which the world's near ripe,
You'll have the younger in the Elder's chair,
Presiding with his ivory front of hope
O'er foreheads clawed by cruel carrion-birds
Of life's experience.''

       '' Pray your blessing, sir,''
Sir Blaise replied good-humoredly, — '' I plucked
A silver hair this morning from my beard,   720
Which left me your inferior.   Would I were
Eighteen and worthy to admonish you !
If young men of your order run before
To see such sights as sexual prejudice
And marriage-law dissolved, — in plainer words,
A general concubinage expressed
In a universal pruriency, — the thing
Is scarce worth running fast for, and you'd gain
By loitering with your elders.''

          '' Ah,'' he said,
'' Who, getting to the top of Pisgah-hill,   730
Can talk with one at bottom of the view,
To make it comprehensible ?   Why, Leigh
Himself, although our ablest man, I said,
Is scarce advanced to see as far as this,
Which some are : he takes up imperfectly
The social question — by one handle — leaves
The rest to trail.   A Christian socialist
Is Romney Leigh, you understand.''

          '' Not I.
I disbelieve in Christian-pagans, much
As you in women-fishes.   If we mix   740
Two colours, we lose both, and make a third
Distinct from either.   Mark you ! to mistake

A colour is the sign of a sick brain,
And mine, I thank the saints, is clear and cool:
A neutral tint is here impossible.
The church, — and by the church I mean, of course,
The catholic, apostolic, mother-church, —
Draws lines as plain and straight as her own walls,
Inside of which are Christian, obviously.   749
And outside . . . dogs.''
                    '' We thank you.   Well I know
The ancient mother-church would fain still bite,
For all her toothless gums, — as Leigh himself
Would fain be a Christian still, for all his wit.
Pass that ; you two may settle it, for me.
You're slow in England.   In a month I learnt
At Göttingen enough philosophy
To stock your English schools for fifty years ;
Pass that, too.   Here alone, I stop you short,
— Supposing a true man like Leigh could stand
Unequal in the stature of his life   760
To the height of his opinions.   Choose a wife
Because of a smooth skin ? — not he, not he !
He'd rail at Venus' self for creaking shoes,
Unless she walked his way of righteousness :
And if he takes a Venus Meretrix
(No imputation on the lady there),
Be sure that, by some sleight of Christian art,
He has metamorphosed and converted her
To a Blessed Virgin.''
                    '' Soft ! '' Sir Blaise drew breath
As if it hurt him, — '' Soft ! no blasphemy,   770
I pray you ! ''
                    '' The first Christians did the thing :
Why not the last ? '' asked he of Göttingen,
With just that shade of sneering on the lip

Compensates for the lagging of the beard, —
" And so the case is. If that fairest fair
Is talked of as the future wife of Leigh,
She's talked of too, at least as certainly,
As Leigh's disciple. You may find her name
On all his missions and commissions, schools,
Asylums, hospitals, — he had her down,   780
With other ladies whom her starry lead
Persuaded from their spheres, to his country-place
In Shropshire, to the famed phalanstery
At Leigh Hall, christianised from Fourier's own
(In which he has planted out his sapling stocks
Of knowledge into social nurseries),
And there, they say, she has tarried half a week,
And milked the cows, and churned, and pressed the
          curd,
And said ' my sister ' to the lowest drab
Of all the assembled castaways ; such girls !   790
Ay, sided with them at the washing-tub —
Conceive, Sir Blaise, those naked perfect arms,
Round glittering arms, plunged elbow-deep in suds,
Like wild swans hid in lilies all a-shake.''

Lord Howe came up.   " What, talking poetry
So near the image of the unfavoring Muse ?
That's you, Miss Leigh : I've watched you half an
          hour
Precisely as I watched the statue called
A Pallas in the Vatican ; — you mind
The face, Sir Blaise ? — intensely calm and sad, 800
As wisdom cut it off from fellowship, —
But *that* spoke louder.   Not a word from *you !*
And these two gentlemen were bold, I marked,
And unabashed by even your silence.''

                              " Ah,"
Said I, " my dear Lord Howe, you shall not speak
To a printing woman who has lost her place
(The sweet safe corner of the household fire
Behind the heads of children), compliments,
As if she were a woman.   We who have clipt
The curls before our eyes may see at least   810
As plain as men do.   Speak out, man to man ;
No compliments, beseech you."
                       " Friend to friend,
Let that be.   We are sad to-night, I saw
(— Good night, Sir Blaise ! ah, Smith — he has
     slipped away),
I saw you across the room, and stayed, Miss Leigh,
To keep a crowd of lion-hunters off,
With faces toward your jungle.   There were three ;
A spacious lady, five feet ten and fat,
Who has the devil in her (and there's room)
For walking to and fro upon the earth,   820
From Chipewa to China ; she requires
Your autograph upon a tinted leaf
'Twixt Queen Pomare's and Emperor Soulouque's.
Pray give it ; she has energies, though fat :
For me, I'd rather see a rick on fire
Than such a woman angry.   Then a youth
Fresh from the backwoods, green as the underboughs,
Asks modestly, Miss Leigh, to kiss your shoe,
And adds, he has an epic in twelve parts,   829
Which when you've read, you'll do it for his boot :
All which I saved you, and absorb next week
Both manuscript and man, — because a lord
Is still more potent than a poetess
With any extreme republican.   Ah, ah,
You smile, at last, then."

           '' Thank you.''
                '' Leave the smile.
I'll lose the thanks for't, — ay, and throw you in
My transatlantic girl, with golden eyes,
That draw you to her splendid whiteness as
The pistil of a water-lily draws,
Adust with gold.   Those girls across the sea   840
Are tyrannously pretty, — and I swore
(She seemed to me an innocent, frank girl)
To bring her to you for a woman's kiss,
Not now, but on some other day or week :
— We'll call it perjury ; I give her up.''

'' No, bring her.''
           '' Now,'' said he, '' you make it hard
To touch such goodness with a grimy palm.
I thought to tease you well, and fret you cross,
And steel myself, when rightly vexed with you,
For telling you a thing to tease you more.''   850

'' Of Romney ? ''
         '' No, no ; nothing worse,'' he cried,
'' Of Romney Leigh than what is buzzed about, —
That *he* is taken in an eye-trap too,
Like many half as wise.   The thing I mean
Refers to you, not him.''
             '' Refers to me.''
He echoed, — '' Me !   You sound it like a stone
Dropped down a dry well very listlessly
By one who never thinks about the toad
Alive at the bottom.   Presently perhaps   859
You'll   sound   your   ' me '   more proudly — till   I
    shrink.''

"Lord Howe's the toad, then, in this question?"
"Brief,

We'll take it graver.   Give me sofa-room,
And quiet hearing.   You know Eglinton,
John Eglinton, of Eglinton in Kent?"

"Is *he* the toad? — he's rather like the snail,
Known chiefly for the house upon his back:
Divide the man and house — you kill the man;
That's Eglinton of Eglinton, Lord Howe."

He answered grave.   "A reputable man,
An excellent landlord of the olden stamp,   870
If somewhat slack in new philanthropies,
Who keeps his birthdays with a tenants' dance,
Is hard upon them when they miss the church
Or hold their children back from catechism,
But not ungentle when the agèd poor
Pick sticks at hedge-sides: nay, I've heard him say
'The old dame has a twinge because she stoops;
That's punishment enough for felony.'"

"O tender-hearted landlord! may I take
My long lease with him, when the time arrives   880
For gathering winter-faggots!"
                                        "He likes art,
Buys books and pictures . . . of a certain kind;
Neglects no patent duty; a good son" . . .

"To a most obedient mother.   Born to wear
His father's shoes, he wears her husband's too:
Indeed I've heard it's touching.   Dear Lord Howe,
You shall not praise *me* so against your heart,
When I'm at worst for praise and faggots."

                                        " Be
Less bitter with me, for . . . in short," he said,
" I have a letter, which he urged me so   890
To bring you . . . I could scarcely choose but
      yield ;
Insisting that a new love, passing through
The hand of an old friendship, caught from it
Some reconciling odour."

                              " Love, you say ?
My lord, I cannot love : I only find
The rhyme for love, — and that's not love, my lord.
Take back your letter."

                         " Pause : you'll read it first ? "

" I will not read it : it is stereotyped ;
The same he wrote to, — anybody's name,
Anne Blythe the actress, when she died so true, 900
A duchess fainted in a private box :
Pauline the dancer, after the great *pas*
In which her little feet winked overhead
Like other fire-flies, and amazed the pit :
Or Baldinacci, when her F in alt
Had touched the silver tops of heaven itself
With such a pungent spirit-dart, the Queen
Laid softly, each to each, her white-gloved palms,
And sighed for joy : or else (I thank your friend)
Aurora Leigh, — when some indifferent rhymes, 910
Like those the boys sang round the holy ox
On Memphis-highway, chance perhaps to set
Our Apis-public lowing.   Oh, he wants,
Instead of any worthy wife at home,
A star upon his stage of Eglinton ?
Advise him that he is not overshrewd
In being so little modest : a dropped star

Makes bitter waters, says a Book I've read, —
And there's his unread letter."

                     " My dear friend,"

Lord Howe began . . .

             In haste I tore the phrase. 920
" You mean your friend of Eglinton, or me ? "

" I mean you, you," he answered with some fire.
" A happy life means prudent compromise ;
The tare runs through the farmer's garnered sheaves,
And though the gleaner's apron holds pure wheat
We count her poorer. Tare with wheat, we cry,
And good with drawbacks. You, you love your art,
And, certain of vocation, set your soul
On utterance. Only, in this world we have made
(They say God made it first, but if He did   930
'Twas so long since, and, since, we have spoiled it so,
He scarce would know it, if He looked this way,
From hells we preach of, with the flames blown out),
— In this bad, twisted, topsy-turvy world
Where all the heaviest wrongs get uppermost, —
In this uneven, unfostering England here,
Where ledger-strokes and sword-strokes count indeed,
But soul-strokes merely tell upon the flesh
They strike from, — it is hard to stand for art,
Unless some golden tripod from the sea   940
Be fished up, by Apollo's divine chance,
To throne such feet as yours, my prophetess,
At Delphi. Think, — the god comes down as fierce
As twenty bloodhounds, shakes you, strangles you,
Until the oracular shriek shall ooze in froth !
At best 'tis not all ease, — at worst too hard :
A place to stand on is a 'vantage gained,
And here's your tripod. To be plain, dear friend,

You're poor, except in what you richly give ;
You labour for your own bread painfully   950
Or ere you pour our wine.   For art's sake, pause.''

I answered slow, — as some wayfaring man,
Who feels himself at night too far from home,
Makes steadfast face against the bitter wind.
'' Is art so less a thing than virtue is,
That artists first must cater for their ease
Or ever they make issue past themselves
To generous use ?   Alas, and is it so
That we, who would be somewhat clean, must sweep
Our ways as well as walk them, and no friend   960
Confirm us nobly, — ' Leave results to God,
But you, be clean ?'   What ! 'prudent compromise
Makes acceptable life,' you say instead,
You, you, Lord Howe ? — in things indifferent, well.
For instance, compromise the wheaten bread
For rye, the meat for lentils, silk for serge,
And sleep on down, if needs, for sleep on straw ;
But there, end compromise.   I will not bate
One artist-dream on straw or down, my lord,
Nor pinch my liberal soul, though I be poor,   970
Nor cease to love high, though I live thus low.''

So speaking, with less anger in my voice
Than sorrow, I rose quickly to depart ;
While he, thrown back upon the noble shame
Of such high-stumbling natures, murmured words,
The right words after wrong ones.   Ah, the man
Is worthy, but so given to entertain
Impossible plans of superhuman life, —
He sets his virtues on so raised a shelf,
To keep them at the grand millennial height,   980

He has to mount a stool to get at them;
And, meantime, lives on quite the common way,
With everybody's morals.
                As we passed,
Lord Howe insisting that his friendly arm
Should oar me across the sparkling brawling stream
Which swept from room to room, — we fell at once
On Lady Waldemar. "Miss Leigh," she said,
And gave me such a smile, so cold and bright,
As if she tried it in a 'tiring glass
And liked it, "all to-night I've strained at you   990
As babes at baubles held up out of reach
By spiteful nurses ('Never snatch,' they say),
And there you sat, most perfectly shut in
By good Sir Blaise and clever Mister Smith
And then our dear Lord Howe! at last indeed
I almost snatched. I have a world to speak
About your cousin's place in Shropshire, where
I've been to see his work . . . our work, — you heard
I went? . . . and of a letter yesterday,
In which if I should read a page or two   1000
You might feel interest, though you're locked of course
In literary toil. — You'll like to hear
Your last book lies at the phalanstery,
As judged innocuous for the elder girls
And younger women who still care for books.
We all must read, you see, before we live,
Till slowly the ineffable light comes up
And, as it deepens, drowns the written word, —
So said your cousin, while we stood and felt
A sunset from his favourite beech-tree seat.   1010
He might have been a poet if he would,
But then he saw the higher thing at once

And climbed to it.   I think he looks well now,
Has quite got over that unfortunate . . .
Ah, ah . . . I know it moved you.   Tender-heart !
You took a liking to the wretched girl.
Perhaps you thought the marriage suitable,
Who knows ? a poet hankers for romance,
And so on.   As for Romney Leigh, 'tis sure
He never loved her, — never.   By the way,   1020
You have not heard of *her* . . . ? quite out of sight,
And out of saving ? lost in every sense ?''

She might have gone on talking half an hour
And I stood still, and cold, and pale, I think,
As a garden-statue a child pelts with snow
For pretty pastime.   Every now and then
I put in '' yes '' or '' no,'' I scarce knew why ;
The blind man walks wherever the dog pulls,   1028
And so I answered.   Till Lord Howe broke in :
'' What penance takes the wretch who interrupts
The talk of charming women ?   I, at last,
Must brave it.   Pardon, Lady Waldemar,
The lady on my arm is tired, unwell,
And loyally I've promised she shall say
No harder word this evening than . . . good-night ;
The rest her face speaks for her.'' — Then we went.

And I breathe large at home.   I drop my cloak,
Unclasp my girdle, loose the band that ties
My hair . . . now could I but unloose my soul !
We are sepulchred alive in this close world,   1040
And want more room.
                              The charming woman there —
This reckoning up and writing down her talk
Affects me singularly.   How she talked

To pain me ! woman's spite. — You wear steel-mail :
A woman takes a housewife from her breast
And plucks the delicatest needle out
As 'twere a rose, and pricks you carefully
'Neath nails, 'neath eyelids, in your nostrils, — say,
A beast would roar so tortured, — but a man,
A human creature, must not, shall not flinch,   1050
No, not for shame.
                         What vexes, after all,
Is just that such as she, with such as I,
Knows how to vex.   Sweet heaven, she takes me up
As if she had fingered me and dog-eared me
And spelled me by the fireside half a life !
She knows my turns, my feeble points. —What then ?
The knowledge of a thing implies the thing ;
Of course, she found *that* in me, she saw *that*,
Her pencil underscored *this* for a fault,   1059
And I, still ignorant.   Shut the book up, — close !
And crush that beetle in the leaves.
                                   O heart,
At last we shall grow hard too, like the rest,
And call it self-defence because we are soft.

And after all, now . . . why should I be pained
That Romney Leigh, my cousin, should espouse
This Lady Waldemar ?   And, say, she held
Her newly-blossomed gladness in my face, . . .
'Twas natural surely, if not generous,
Considering how, when winter held her fast,   1069
I helped the frost with mine, and pained her more
Than she pains me.   Pains me ! — but wherefore
       pained ?
'Tis clear my cousin Romney wants a wife, —
So, good ! — The man's need of the woman, here,

Is greater than the woman's of the man,
And easier served ; for where the man discerns
A sex (ah, ah, the man can generalise,
Said he), we see but one, ideally
And really : where we yearn to lose ourselves
And melt like white pearls in another's wine,
He seeks to double himself by what he loves,   1080
And make his drink more costly by our pearls.
At board, at bed, at work and holiday,
It is not good for man to be alone,
And that's his way of thinking, first and last,
And thus my cousin Romney wants a wife.
But then my cousin sets his dignity
On personal virtue.   If he understands
By love, like others, self-aggrandisement,
It is that he may verily be great   1089
By doing rightly and kindly.   Once he thougnt,
For charitable ends set duly forth
In Heaven's white judgment-book, to marry . . .
    ah,
We'll call her name Aurora Leigh, although
She's changed since then ! — and once, for social
    ends,
Poor Marian Erle, my sister Marian Erle,
My woodland sister, sweet maid Marian,
Whose memory moans on in me like the wind
Through ill-shut casements, making me more sad
Than ever I find reasons for.   Alas,
Poor pretty plaintive face, embodied ghost !   1100
He finds it easy then, to clap thee off
From pulling at his sleeve and book and pen, —
He locks thee out at night into the cold
Away from butting with thy horny eyes
Against his crystal dreams, that now he's strong

To love anew ? that Lady Waldemar
Succeeds my Marian ?
                         After all, why not ?
He loved not Marian, more than once he loved
Aurora.   If he loves at last that Third,
Albeit she prove as slippery as spilt oil   1110
On marble floors, I will not augur him
Ill-luck for that.   Good love, howe'er ill-placed,
Is better for a man's soul in the end,
Than if he loved ill what deserves love well.
A pagan, kissing for a step of Pan
The wild-goat's hoof-print on the loamy down,
Exceeds our modern thinker who turns back
The strata . . . granite, limestone, coal, and clay,
Concluding coldly with " Here's law ! where's
          God ? "   1119

And then at worst, — if Romney loves her not,—
At worst — if he's incapable of love,
Which may be — then indeed, for such a man
Incapable of love, she's good enough ;
For she, at worst too, is a woman still
And loves him . . . as the sort of woman can.

My loose long hair began to burn and creep,
Alive to the very ends, about my knees :
I swept it backward as the wind sweeps flame, 1128
With the passion of my hands.   Ah, Romney laughed
One day . . . (how full the memories come up !)
" — Your Florence fire-flies live on in your hair,"
He said, " it gleams so."   Well, I wrung them out,
My fire-flies ; made a knot as hard as life
Of those loose, soft, impracticable curls,

And then sat down and thought . . . " She shall
    not think
Her thought of me," — and drew my desk and
    wrote.

" Dear Lady Waldemar, I could not speak
With people round me, nor can sleep to-night
And not speak, after the great news I heard
Of you and of my cousin.   May you be   1140
Most happy ; and the good he meant the world
Replenish his own life.   Say what I say,
And let my word be sweeter for your mouth,
As you are *you* . . . I only Aurora Leigh."
That's quiet, guarded : though she hold it up
Against the light, she'll not see through it more
Than lies there to be seen.   So much for pride ;
And now for peace, a little.   Let me stop
All writing back . . . " Sweet thanks, my sweetest
    friend,
You've made more joyful my great joy itself."   1150
— No, that's too simple ! she would twist it thus,
" My joy would still be as sweet as thyme in drawers,
However shut up in the dark and dry ;
But violets, aired and dewed by love like yours,
Out-smell all thyme : we keep that in our clothes,
But drop the other down our bosoms till
They smell like — " . . . ah, I see her writing
    back
Just so.   She'll make a nosegay of her words,
And tie it with blue ribbons at the end
To suit a poet ; — pshaw !
                                And then we'll have   1160
The call to church, the broken, sad, bad dream
Dreamed out at last, the marriage-vow complete

With the marriage breakfast ; praying in white gloves,
Drawn off in haste for drinking pagan toasts
In somewhat stronger wine than any sipped
By gods since Bacchus had his way with grapes.

A postscript stops all that and rescues me.
" You need not write.   I have been overworked,
And think of leaving London, England even,
And hastening to get nearer to the sun   1170
Where men sleep better.   So, adieu." — I fold
And seal, —— and now I'm out of all the coil ;
I breathe now, I spring upward like a branch
The ten-years school-boy with a crooked stick
May pull down to his level in search of nuts,
But cannot hold a moment.   How we twang
Back on the blue sky, and assert our height,
While he stares after !   Now, the wonder seems
That I could wrong myself by such a doubt.
We poets always have uneasy hearts,   1180
Because our hearts, large-rounded as the globe,
Can turn but one side to the sun at once.
We are used to dip our artist-hands in gall
And potash, trying potentialities
Of alternated colour, till at last
We get confused, and wonder for our skin
How nature tinged it first.   Well — here's the true
Good flesh-colour ; I recognise my hand, —
Which Romney Leigh may clasp as just a friend's,
And keep his clean.
                    And now, my Italy.   1190
Alas, if we could ride with naked souls
And make no noise and pay no price at all,
I would have seen thee sooner, Italy,
For still I have heard thee crying through my life,

Thou piercing silence of ecstatic graves,
Men call that name !

                     But even a witch to-day
Must melt down golden pieces in the nard
Wherewith to anoint her broomstick ere she rides ;
And poets evermore are scant of gold,
And if they find a piece behind the door   1200
It turns by sunset to a withered leaf.
The Devil himself scarce trusts his patented
Gold-making art to any who make rhymes,
But culls his Faustus from philosophers
And not from poets.   " Leave my Job,'' said God ;
And so the Devil leaves him without pence,
And poverty proves plainly special grace.
In these new, just, administrative times
Men clamour for an order of merit : why ?
Here's black bread on the table and no wine !   1210

At least I am a poet in being poor,
Thank God.   I wonder if the manuscript
Of my long poem, if 'twere sold outright,
Would fetch enough to buy me shoes to go
Afoot (thrown in, the necessary patch
For the other side the Alps) ?   It cannot be.
I fear that I must sell this residue
Of my father's books, although the Elzevirs
Have fly-leaves overwritten by his hand
In faded notes as thick and fine and brown   1220
As cobwebs on a tawny monument
Of the old Greeks — *conferenda hæc cum his* —
Corruptè citat — *lege potiùs,*
And so on, in the scholar's regal way
Of giving judgment on the parts of speech,

As if he sat on all twelve thrones up-piled,
Arraigning Israel.   Ay, but books and notes
Must go together.   And this Proclus too,
In these dear quaint contracted Grecian types,
Fantastically crumpled like his thoughts   1230
Which would not seem too plain ; you go round
        twice
For one step forward, then you take it back
Because you're somewhat giddy ; there's the rule
For Proclus.   Ah, I stained this middle leaf
With pressing in't my Florence iris-bell,
Long stalk and all : my father chided me
For that stain of blue blood, — I recollect
The peevish turn his voice took, — " Silly girls,
Who plant their flowers in our philosophy
To make it fine, and only spoil the book !   1240
No more of it, Aurora."   Yes — no more !
Ah, blame of love, that's sweeter than all praise
Of those who love not ! 'tis so lost to me,
I cannot, in such beggared life, afford
To lose my Proclus,— not for Florence even.

The kissing Judas, Wolff, shall go instead,
Who builds us such a royal book as this
To honour a chief-poet, folio-built,
And writes above " The house of Nobody ! "
Who floats in cream, as rich as any sucked   1250
From Juno's breasts, the broad Homeric lines,
And, while with their spondaic prodigious mouths
They lap the lucent margins as babe-gods,
Proclaims them bastards.   Wolff's an atheist :
And if the Iliad fell out, as he says,
By mere fortuitous concourse of old songs,
Conclude as much too for the universe.

That Wolff, those Platos : sweep the upper shelves
As clean as this, and so I am almost rich,
Which means, not forced to think of being poor 1260
In sight of ends.　To-morrow : no delay.
I'll wait in Paris till good Carrington
Dispose of such and, having chaffered for
My book's price with the publisher, direct
All proceeds to me.　Just a line to ask
His help.

　　　　　　And now I come, my Italy,
My own hills !　Are you 'ware of me, my hills,
How I burn toward you ? do you feel to-night
The urgency and yearning of my soul,
As sleeping mothers feel the sucking babe　　1270
And smile ? — Nay, not so much as when in heat
Vain lightnings catch at your inviolate tops
And tremble while ye are steadfast.　Still ye go
Your own determined, calm, indifferent way
Toward sunrise, shade by shade, and light by light,
Of all the grand progression nought left out,
As if God verily made you for yourselves
And would not interrupt your life with ours.

SIXTH BOOK.

THE English have a scornful insular way
Of calling the French light.　The levity
Is in the judgment only, which yet stands,
For say a foolish thing but oft enough
(And here's the secret of a hundred creeds,
Men get opinions as boys learn to spell,
By reiteration chiefly), the same thing
Shall pass at last for absolutely wise,

And not with fools exclusively.   And so
We say the French are light, as if we said   10
The cat mews or the milch-cow gives us milk :
Say rather, cats are milked and milch-cows mew ;
For what is lightness but inconsequence,
Vague fluctuation 'twixt effect and cause
Compelled by neither ?   Is the bullet light
That dashes from the gun-mouth, while the eye
Winks and the heart beats one, to flatten itself
To a wafer on the white speck on a wall
A hundred paces off ?   Even so direct,
So sternly undivertible of aim,   20
Is this French people.
              All, idealists
Too absolute and earnest, with them all
The idea of a knife cuts real flesh ;
And still, devouring the safe interval
Which Nature placed between the thought and act
With those two fiery and impatient souls,
They threaten conflagration to the world,
And rush with most unscrupulous logic on
Impossible practice.   Set your orators
To blow upon them with loud windy mouths,   30
Through watchword phrases, jest or sentiment,
Which drive our burly brutal English mobs
Like so much chaff, whichever way they blow, —
This light French people will not thus be driven.
They turn indeed, — but then they turn upon
Some central pivot of their thought and choice,
And veer out by the force of holding fast.
That's hard to understand, for Englishmen
Unused to abstract questions, and untrained
To trace the involutions, valve by valve,   40
In each orbed bulb-root of a general truth,

And mark what subtly fine integument
Divides opposed compartments.   Freedom's self
Comes concrete to us, to be understood,
Fixed in a feudal form incarnately
To suit our ways of thought and reverence,
The special form, with us, being still the thing.
With us, I say, though I'm of Italy
By mother's birth and grave, by father's grave
And memory ; let it be — a poet's heart   50
Can swell to a pair of nationalities,
However ill-lodged in a woman's breast.

And so I am strong to love this noble France,
This poet of the nations, who dreams on
And wails on (while the household goes to wreck)
For ever, after some ideal good, —
Some equal poise of sex, some unvowed love
Inviolate, some spontaneous brotherhood,
Some wealth that leaves none poor and finds none
        tired,
Some freedom of the many that respects   60
The wisdom of the few.   Heroic dreams !
Sublime, to dream so ; natural, to wake :
And sad, to use such lofty scaffoldings,
Erected for the building of a church,
To build instead a brothel or a prison —
May God save France !
                    And if at last she sighs
Her great soul up into a great man's face,
To flush his temples out so gloriously
That few dare carp at Cæsar for being bald,
What then ? — this Cæsar represents, not reigns,   70
And is no despot, though twice absolute :
This Head has all the people for a heart ;

This purple's lined with the democracy, —
Now let him see to it ! for a rent within
Would leave irreparable rags without.

A serious riddle : find such anywhere
Except in France ; and when 'tis found in France,
Be sure to read it rightly.   So, I mused
Up and down, up and down, the terraced streets,
The glittering boulevards, the white colonnades   80
Of fair fantastic Paris who wears trees
Like plumes, as if man made them, spire and tower
As if they had grown by nature, tossing up
Her fountains in the sunshine of the squares,
As if in beauty's game she tossed the dice,
Or blew the silver down-balls of her dreams
To sow futurity with seeds of thought
And count the passage of her festive hours.

The city swims in verdure, beautiful
As Venice on the waters, the sea-swan.   90
What bosky gardens dropped in close-walled courts
Like plums in ladies' laps who start and laugh :
What miles of streets that run on after trees,
Still carrying all the necessary shops,
Those open caskets with the jewels seen !
And trade is art, and art's philosophy,
In Paris.   There's a silk for instance, there,
As worth an artist's study for the folds
As that bronze opposite ! nay, the bronze has faults,
Art's here too artful, — conscious as a maid   100
Who leans to mark her shadow on the wall
Until she lose a vantage in her step.
Yet Art walks forward, and knows where to walk ;
The artists also are idealists,

Too absolute for nature, logical
To austerity in the application of
The special theory, — not a soul content
To paint a crooked pollard and an ass,
As the English will because they find it so
And like it somehow. — There the old Tuileries 110
Is pulling its high cap down on its eyes,
Confounded, conscience-stricken, and amazed
By the apparition of a new fair face
In those devouring mirrors.   Through the grate
Within the gardens, what a heap of babes,
Swept up like leaves beneath the chestnut-trees
From every street and alley of the town,
By ghosts perhaps that blow too bleak this way
A-looking for their heads ! dear pretty babes,
I wish them luck to have their ball-play out   120
Before the next change.   Here the air is thronged
With statues poised upon their columns fine,
As if to stand a moment were a feat,
Against that blue !   What squares, — what breathing-
        room
For a nation that runs fast, — ay, runs against
The dentist's teeth at the corner in pale rows,
Which grin at progress, in an epigram.

I walked the day out, listening to the chink
Of the first Napoleon's bones in his second grave,
By victories guarded 'neath the golden dome   130
That caps all Paris like a bubble.   "Shall
These dry bones live ?" thought Louis Philippe once,
And lived to know.   Herein is argument
For kings and politicians, but still more
For poets, who bear buckets to the well
Of ampler draught.

These crowds are very good
For meditation (when we are very strong)
Though love of beauty makes us timorous,
And draws us backward from the coarse town-sights
To count the daisies upon dappled fields   140
And hear the streams bleat on among the hills
In innocent and indolent repose,
While still with silken elegiac thoughts
We wind out from us the distracting world
And die into the chrysalis of a man,
And leave the best that may, to come of us,
In some brown moth.   I would be bold and bear
To look into the swarthiest face of things,
For God's sake who has made them.

Six days' work ;
The last day shutting 'twixt its dawn and eve   150
The whole work bettered of the previous five !
Since God collected and resumed in man
The firmaments, the strata, and the lights,
Fish, fowl, and beast, and insect, — all their trains
Of various life caught back upon His arm,
Reorganised, and constituted MAN,
The microcosm, the adding up of works, —
Within whose fluttering nostrils, then at last
Consummating Himself the Maker sighed,
As some strong winner at the foot-race sighs   160
Touching the goal.
Humanity is great ;
And, if I would not rather pore upon
An ounce of common, ugly, human dust,
An artisan's palm or a peasant's brow,
Unsmooth, ignoble, save to me and God,
Than track old Nilus to his silver roots,

Or wait on all the changes of the moon
Among the mountain-peaks of Thessaly
(Until her magic crystal round itself
For many a witch to see in) — set it down   170
As weakness, — strength by no means.   How is this,
That men of science, osteologists
And surgeons, beat some poets in respect
For Nature, — count nought common or unclean,
Spend raptures upon perfect specimens
Of indurated veins, distorted joints,
Or beautiful new cases of curved spine,
While we, we are shocked at nature's falling off,
We dare to shrink back from her warts and blains,
We will not, when she sneezes, look at her,   180
Not even to say " God bless her " ?   That's our
          wrong ;
For that, she will not trust us often with
Her larger sense of beauty and desire,
But tethers us to a lily or a rose
And bids us diet on the dew inside,
Left ignorant that the hungry beggar-boy
(Who stares unseen against our absent eyes,
And wonders at the gods that we must be,
To pass so careless for the oranges !)
Bears yet a breastful of a fellow-world   190
To this world, undisparaged, undespoiled,
And (while we scorn him for a flower or two,
As being, Heaven help us, less poetical)
Contains himself both flowers and firmaments
And surging seas and aspectable stars
And all that we would push him out of sight
In order to see nearer.   Let us pray
God's grace to keep God's image in repute,
That so, the poet and philanthropist

(Even I and Romney) may stand side by side,   200
Because we both stand face to face with men,
Contemplating the people in the rough,
Yet each so follow a vocation, his
And mine.
        I walked on, musing with myself
On life and art, and whether after all
A larger metaphysics might not help
Our physics, a completer poetry
Adjust our daily life and vulgar wants
More fully than the special outside plans,
Phalansteries, material institutes,   210
The civil conscriptions and lay monasteries
Preferred by modern thinkers, as they thought
The bread of man indeed made all his life,
And washing seven times in the " People's Baths "
Were sovereign for a people's leprosy,
Still leaving out the essential prophet's word
That comes in power. On which, we thunder
    down,
We prophets, poets, — Virtue's in the *word!*
The maker burnt the darkness up with His,
To inaugurate the use of vocal life ;   220
And, plant a poet's word even, deep enough
In any man's breast, looking presently
For offshoots, you have done more for the man
Than if you dressed him in a broadcloth coat
And warmed his Sunday pottage at your fire.
Yet Romney leaves me . . .
           God ! what face is that ?
O Romney, O Marian !
          Walking on the quays
And pulling thoughts to pieces leisurely,
As if I caught at grasses in a field

And bit them slow between my absent lips   230
And shred them with my hands . . .

What face is that?
What a face, what a look, what a likeness!   Full on
    mine
The sudden blow of it came down, till all
My blood swam, my eyes dazzled.   Then I
    sprang . . .

It was as if a meditative man
Were dreaming out a summer afternoon
And watching gnats a-prick upon a pond,
When something floats up suddenly, out there,
Turns over . . . a dead face, known once
    alive . . .
So old, so new! it would be dreadful now   240
To lose the sight and keep the doubt of this:
He plunges — ha! he has lost it in the splash.

I plunged — I tore the crowd up, either side,
And rushed on, forward, forward, after her.
Her? whom?

A woman sauntered slow in front,
Munching an apple, — she left off amazed
As if I had snatched it: that's not she, at least.
A man walked arm-linked with a lady veiled,
Both heads dropped closer than the need of talk:
They started; he forgot her with his face,   250
And she, herself, and clung to him as if
My look were fatal.   Such a stream of folk,
And all with cares and business of their own!
I ran the whole quay down against their eyes;
No Marian; nowhere Marian.   Almost, now,
I could call Marian, Marian, with the shriek

Of desperate creatures calling for the Dead.
Where is she, was she ? was she anywhere ?
I stood still, breathless, gazing, straining out
In every uncertain distance, till at last   260
A gentleman abstracted as myself
Came full against me, then resolved the clash
In voluble excuses, — obviously
Some learned member of the Institute
Upon his way there, walking, for his health,
While meditating on the last " Discourse ; "
Pinching the empty air 'twixt finger and thumb,
From which the snuff being ousted by that shock
Defiled his snow-white waistcoat duly pricked
At the button-hole with honourable red ;   270
" Madame, your pardon," — there he swerved from me
A metre, as confounded as he had heard
That Dumas would be chosen to fill up
The next chair vacant, by his " men *in us*."
Since when was genius found respectable ?
It passes in its place, indeed,   which means
The seventh floor back, or else the hospital :
Revolving pistols are ingenious things.
But prudent men (Academicians are)
Scarce keep them in the cupboard next the prunes. 280

And so, abandoned to a bitter mirth,
I loitered to my inn.   O world, O world,
O jurists, rhymers, dreamers, what you please,
We play a weary game of hide-and-seek !
We shape a figure of our fantasy,
Call nothing something, and run after it
And lose it, lose ourselves too in the search,
Till clash against us comes a somebody

Who also has lost something and is lost,
Philosopher against philanthropist,   290
Academician against poet, man
Against woman, against the living the dead, —
Then home, with a bad headache and worse jest !

To change the water for my heliotropes
And yellow roses.   Paris has such flowers ;
But England, also.   'Twas a yellow rose,
By that south window of the little house,
My cousin Romney gathered with his hand
On all my birthdays for me, save the last ;
And then I shook the tree too rough, too rough,   300
For roses to stay after.
                              Now, my maps.
I must not linger here from Italy
Till the last nightingale is tired of song,
And the last fire-fly dies off in the maize.
My soul's in haste to leap into the sun
And scorch and seethe itself to a finer mood,
Which here, in this chill north, is apt to stand
Too stiffly in former moulds.
                              That face persists,
It floats up, it turns over in my mind,
As like to Marian as one dead is like   310
The same alive.   In very deed a face
And not a fancy, though it vanished so ;
The small fair face between the darks of hair,
I used to liken, when I saw her first,
To a point of moonlit water down a well :
The low brow, the frank space between the eyes,
Which always had the brown, pathetic look
Of a dumb creature who had been beaten once
And never since was easy with the world.

Ah, ah — now I remember perfectly   320
Those eyes, to-day, — how overlarge they seemed,
As if some patient, passionate despair
(Like a coal dropped and forgot on tapestry,
Which slowly burns a widening circle out)
Had burnt them larger, larger.   And those eyes,
To-day, I do remember, saw me too,
As I saw them, with conscious lids astrain
In recognition.   Now a fantasy,
A simple shade of image of the brain,
Is merely passive, does not retro-act,   330
Is seen, but sees not.
                        'Twas a real face,
Perhaps a real Marian.
                        Which being so,
I ought to write to Romney, " Marian's here ;
Be comforted for Marian."
                        My pen fell,
My hands struck sharp together, as hands do
Which hold at nothing.   Can I write to *him*
A half-truth ? can I keep my own soul blind
To the other half, . . . the worse ? What are our
     souls,
If still, to run on straight a sober pace
Nor start at every pebble or dead leaf,   340
They must wear blinkers, ignore facts, suppress
Six tenths of the road ?   Confront the truth, my soul !
And oh, as truly as that was Marian's face,
The arms of that same Marian clasped a thing
. . . Not hid so well beneath the scanty shawl,
I cannot name it now for what it was.

A child.   Small business has a castaway
Like Marian with that crown of prosperous wives

At which the gentlest she grows arrogant   349
And says " My child."   Who finds an emerald ring
On a beggar's middle finger and requires
More testimony to convict a thief?
A child's too costly for so mere a wretch ;
She filched it somewhere, and it means, with her,
Instead of honour, blessing, merely shame.

I cannot write to Romney, " Here she is,
Here's Marian found !   I'll set you on her track :
I saw her here, in Paris, . . . and her child.
She put away your love two years ago,
But, plainly, not to starve.   You suffered then ;   360
And, now that you've forgot her utterly
As any last year's annual, in whose place
You've planted a thick-flowering evergreen,
I choose, being kind, to write and tell you this
To make you wholly easy — she's not dead,
But only . . . damned."
                                        Stop there : I go too fast ;
I'm cruel like the rest, — in haste to take
The first stir in the arras for a rat,
And set my barking, biting thoughts upon't.   369
— A child ! what then ? Suppose a neighbour's sick,
And asked her, " Marian, carry out my child
In this Spring air," — I punish her for that ?
Or say, the child should hold her round the neck
For good child-reasons, that he liked it so
And would not leave her — she had winning ways —
I brand her therefore that she took the child ?
Not so.
                I will not write to Romney Leigh,
For now he's happy, — and she may indeed
Be guilty, — and the knowledge of her fault   379

Would draggle his smooth time.   But I, whose days
Are not so fine they cannot bear the rain,
And who moreover having seen her face
Must see it again, . . . *will* see it, by my hopes
Of one day seeing heaven too.   The police
Shall track her, hound her, ferret their own soil ;
We'll dig this Paris to its catacombs
But certainly we'll find her, have her out,
And save her, if she will or will not — child
Or no child, — if a child, then one to save !

The long weeks passed on without consequence.   390
As easy find a footstep on the sand
The morning after spring-tide, as the trace
Of Marian's feet between the incessant surfs
Of this live flood.   She may have moved this way, —
But so the star-fish does, and crosses out
The dent of her small shoe.   The foiled police
Renounce me.   " Could they find a girl and child,
No other signalment but girl and child ?
No data shown but noticeable eyes
And hair in masses, low upon the brow,   400
As if it were an iron crown and pressed ?
Friends heighten, and suppose they specify :
Why, girls with hair and eyes are everywhere
In Paris ; they had turned me up in vain
No Marian Erle indeed, but certainly
Mathildes, Justines, Victoires, . . . or, if I sought
The English, Betsis, Saras, by the score.
They might as well go out into the fields
To find a speckled bean, that's somehow speckled,
And somewhere in the pod."— They left me so.
Shall *I* leave Marian ? have I dreamed a dream ? 411

— I thank God I have found her ! I must say
"Thank God," for finding her, although 'tis true
I find the world more sad and wicked for't.
But she —
    I'll write about her, presently.
My hand's a-tremble, as I had just caught up
My heart to write with, in the place of it.
At least you'd take these letters to be writ
At sea, in storm ! — wait now. . . .
        A simple chance
Did all. I could not sleep last night, and, tired 420
Of turning on my pillow and harder thoughts,
Went out at early morning, when the air
Is delicate with some last starry touch,
To wander through the Market-place of Flowers
(The prettiest haunt in Paris), and make sure
At worst that there were roses in the world.
So wandering, musing, with the artist's eye,
That keeps the shade-side of the thing it loves,
Half-absent, whole-observing, while the crowd
Of young, vivacious, and black-braided heads 430
Dipped, quick as finches in a blossomed tree,
Among the nosegays, cheapening this and that
In such a cheerful twitter of rapid speech, —
My heart leapt in me, startled by a voice
That slowly, faintly, with long breaths that marked
The interval between the wish and word,
Inquired in stranger's French, "Would *that* be much,
That branch of flowering mountain-gorse ? " — " So
   much ?
Too much for me, then !" turning the face round
So close upon me that I felt the sigh   440
It turned with.
    "Marian, Marian !" — face to face —

" Marian ! I find you.   Shall I let you go ? "
I held her two slight wrists with both my hands ;
" Ah Marian, Marian, can I let you go ? "
— She fluttered from me like a cyclamen,
As white, which taken in a sudden wind
Beats on against the palisade.— " Let pass,"
She said at last.   " I will not," I replied ;
" I lost my sister Marian many days,
And sought her ever in my walks and prayers,   450
And, now I find her . . . do we throw away
The bread we worked and prayed for,— crumble it
And drop it, . . . to do even so by thee
Whom still I've hungered after more than bread,
My sister Marian ? — can I hurt thee, dear ?
Then why distrust me ?   Never tremble so.
Come with me rather where we'll talk and live,
And none shall vex us.   I've a home for you
And me and no one else."   . . .

       She shook her head.
" A home for you and me and no one else   460
Ill suits one of us ; I prefer to such,
A roof of grass on which a flower might spring,
Less costly to me than the cheapest here ;
And yet I could not, at this hour, afford
A like home even.   That you offer yours,
I thank you.   You are good as heaven itself—
As good as one I knew before. . . . Farewell."
I loosed her hands : —" In *his* name, no farewell ! "
(She stood as if I held her.)   " For his sake,
For his sake, Romney's ! by the good he meant,   470
Ay, always ! by the love he pressed for once,—
And by the grief, reproach, abandonment,
He took in change " . . .

     " He ? — Romney ! who grieved *him* ?

Who had the heart for't? what reproach touched
    him?
Be merciful,— speak quickly."

                        " Therefore come,"
I answered with authority.— " I think
We dare to speak such things and name such names
In the open squares of Paris ! "

                      Not a word
She said, but in a gentle humbled way
(As one who had forgot herself in grief)   480
Turned round and followed closely where I went,
As if I led her by a narrow plank
Across devouring waters, step by step ;
And so in silence we walked on a mile.

And then she stopped : her face was white as wax.
" We go much farther ? "

                   " You are ill," I asked,
" Or tired ? "

            She looked the whiter for her smile.
" There's one at home," she said, " has need of me
By this time,— and I must not let him wait."   489

" Not even," I asked, " to hear of Romney Leigh ? "

" Not even," she said, " to hear of Mister Leigh."

" In that case," I resumed, " I go with you,
And we can talk the same thing there as here.
None waits for me : I have my day to spend."

Her lips moved in a spasm without a sound,—
But then she spoke.   " It shall be as you please ;
And better so — 'tis shorter seen than told :

And though you will not find me worth your pains,
That, even, may be worth some pains to know
For one as good as you are."

Then she led   500

The way, and I, as by a narrow plank
Across devouring waters, followed her,
Stepping by her footsteps, breathing by her breath,
And holding her with eyes that would not slip ;
And so, without a word, we walked a mile,
And so, another mile, without a word.

Until the peopled streets being all dismissed,
House-rows and groups all scattered like a flock,
The market-gardens thickened, and the long
White walls beyond, like spiders' outside threads, 510
Stretched, feeling blindly toward the country-fields,
Through half-built habitations and half-dug
Foundations,— intervals of trenchant chalk
That bit betwixt the grassy uneven turfs
Where goats (vine-tendrils trailing from their mouths)
Stood perched on edges of the cellarage
Which should be, staring as about to leap
To find their coming Bacchus.   All the place
Seemed less a cultivation than a waste.
Men work here, only, — scarce begin to live :   520
All's sad, the country struggling with the town,
Like an untamed hawk upon a strong man's fist,
That beats its wings and tries to get away,
And cannot choose be satisfied so soon
To hop through court-yards with its right foot tied,
The vintage plains and pastoral hills in sight.

We stopped beside a house too high and slim
To stand there by itself, but waiting till

Five others, two on this side, three on that,
Should grow up from the sullen second floor   530
They pause at now, to build it to a row.
The upper windows partly were unglazed
Meantime,— a meagre, unripe house : a line
Of rigid poplars elbowed it behind,
And, just in front, beyond the lime and bricks
That wronged the grass between it and the road,
A great acacia with its slender trunk
And overpoise of multitudinous leaves
(In which a hundred fields might spill their dew
And intense verdure, yet find room enough)   540
Stood reconciling all the place with green.
I followed up the stair upon her step.
She hurried upward, shot across a face,
A woman's, on the landing, — "How now, now !
Is no one to have holidays but you ?
You said an hour, and stayed three hours, I think,
And Julie waiting for your betters here ?
Why if he had waked he might have waked, for me."
— Just murmuring an excusing word, she passed
And shut the rest out with the chamber door,   550
Myself shut in beside her.
                                        'Twas a room
Scarce larger than a grave, and near as bare ;
Two stools, a pallet-bed ; I saw the room :
A mouse could find no sort of shelter in't,
Much less a greater secret ; curtainless, —
The window fixed you with its torturing eye,
Defying you to take a step apart
If peradventure you would hide a thing.
I saw the whole room, I and Marian there
Alone.
                    Alone ?   She threw her bonnet off,   560

Then, sighing as 'twere sighing the last time,
Approached the bed, and drew a shawl away :
You could not peel a fruit you fear to bruise
More calmly and more carefully than so, —
Nor would you find within, a rosier flushed
Pomegranate —

           There he lay upon his back,
The yearling creature, warm and moist with life
To the bottom of his dimples, — to the ends
Of the lovely tumbled curls about his face ;
For since he had been covered over-much   570
To keep him from the light-glare, both his cheeks
Were hot and scarlet as the first live rose
The shepherd's heart-blood ebbed away into
The faster for his love.   And love was here
As instant ; in the pretty baby-mouth,
Shut close as if for dreaming that it sucked,
The little naked feet, drawn up the way
Of nestled birdlings ; everything so soft
And tender, — to the tiny holdfast hands,
Which, closing on a finger into sleep,   580
Had kept the mould of 't.

             While we stood there dumb,
For oh, that it should take such innocence
To prove just guilt, I thought, and stood there dumb,—
The light upon his eyelids pricked them wide,
And, staring out at us with all their blue,
As half perplexed between the angelhood
He had been away to visit in his sleep,
And our most mortal presence, gradually
He saw his mother's face, accepting it
In change for heaven itself with such a smile   590
As might have well been learnt there, — never moved,
But smiled on, in a drowse of ecstasy,

So happy (half with her and half with heaven)
He could not have the trouble to be stirred,
But smiled and lay there.   Like a rose, I said ?
As red and still indeed as any rose,
That blows in all the silence of its leaves,
Content in blowing to fulfil its life.

She leaned above him (drinking him as wine)
In that extremity of love, 'twill pass   600
For agony or rapture, seeing that love
Includes the whole of nature, rounding it
To love . . . no more, — since more can never be
Than just love.   Self-forgot, cast out of self,
And drowning in the transport of the sight,
Her whole pale passionate face, mouth, forehead, eyes,
One gaze, she stood : then, slowly as he smiled
She smiled too, slowly, smiling unaware,
And drawing from his countenance to hers
A fainter red, as if she watched a flame   610
And stood in it a-glow.   "How beautiful,"
Said she.
             I answered, trying to be cold.
(Must sin have compensations, was my thought,
As if it were a holy thing like grief ?
And is a woman to be fooled aside
From putting vice down, with that woman's toy
A baby ?) —— "Ay ! the child is well enough,"
I answered.   "If his mother's palms are clean
They need be glad of course in clasping such ;
But if not, I would rather lay my hand,   620
Were I she, on God's brazen altar-bars
Red-hot with burning sacrificial lambs,
Than touch the sacred curls of such a child."

She plunged her fingers in his clustering locks,
As one who would not be afraid of fire ;
And then with indrawn steady utterance said,
" My lamb, my lamb ! although, through such as
    thou,
The most unclean got courage and approach
To God, once, — now they cannot, even with men,
Find grace enough for pity and gentle words."   630

" My Marian," I made answer, grave and sad,
" The priest who stole a lamb to offer him,
Was still a thief.   And if a woman steals
(Through God's own barrier-hedges of true love,
Which fence out license in securing love)
A child like this, that smiles so in her face,
She is no mother, but a kidnapper,
And he's a dismal orphan, not a son,
Whom all her kisses cannot feed so full
He will not miss hereafter a pure home   640
To live in, a pure heart to lean against,
A pure good mother's name and memory
'To hope by, when the world grows thick and bad
And he feels out for virtue."
                              " Oh," she smiled
With bitter patience, " the child takes his chance ;
Not much worse off in being fatherless
Than I was, fathered.   He will say, belike,
His mother was the saddest creature born ;
He'll say his mother lived so contrary
To joy, that even the kindest, seeing her,   650
Grew sometimes almost cruel : he'll not say
She flew contrarious in the face of God
With bat wings of her vices.   Stole my child, —
My flower of earth, my only flower on earth,

My sweet, my beauty ! " . . . Up she snatched the
     child,
And, breaking on him in a storm of tears,
Drew out her long sobs from their shivering roots,
Until he took it for a game, and stretched
His feet and flapped his eager arms like wings   659
And crowed and gurgled through his infant laugh :
" Mine, mine," she said.   " I have as sure a right
As any glad proud mother in the world,
Who sets her darling down to cut his teeth
Upon her church-ring.   If she talks of law,
I talk of law !   I claim my mother-dues
By law, — the law which now is paramount, —
The common law, by which the poor and weak
Are trodden underfoot by vicious men,
And loathed for ever after by the good.
Let pass !   I did not filch, — I found the child." 670
" You found him, Marian ? "

                              " Ay, I found him where
I found my curse, — in the gutter, with my shame !
What have you, any of you, to say to that,
Who all are happy, and sit safe and high,
And never spoke before to arraign my right
To grief itself ?   What, what, . . . being beaten
     down
By hoofs of maddened oxen into a ditch,
Half-dead, whole mangled, when a girl at last
Breathes, sees . . . and finds there, bedded in her
     flesh
Because of the extremity of the shock,   680
Some coin of price ! . . . and when a good man
     comes
(That's God !   the best men are not quite as good)
And says 'I dropped the coin there : take it you,

And keep it, — it shall pay you for the loss,' —
You all put up your finger — 'See the thief!
' Observe what precious thing she has come to filch.
' How bad those girls are !' Oh, my flower, my
    pet,
I dare forget I have you in my arms
And fly off to be angry with the world,
And fright you, hurt you with my tempers, till   690
You double up your lip ? Why, that indeed
Is bad : a naughty mother !''

                          ''You mistake,''

I interrupted ; '' if I loved you not,
I should not, Marian, certainly be here.''

'' Alas,'' she said, '' you are so very good ;
And yet I wish indeed you had never come
To make me sob until I vex the child.
It is not wholesome for these pleasure-plats
To be so early watered by our brine.
And then, who knows ? he may not like me now 700
As well, perhaps, as ere he saw me fret, —
One's ugly fretting ! he has eyes the same
As angels, but he cannot see as deep,
And so I've kept for ever in his sight
A sort of smile to please him, — as you place
A green thing from the garden in a cup,
To make believe it grows there. Look, my sweet,
My cowslip-ball ! we've done with that cross face,
And here's the face come back you used to like. 709
Ah, ah ! he laughs ! he likes me. Ah, Miss Leigh,
You're great and pure ; but were you purer still, —
As if you had walked, we'll say, no otherwhere
Than up and down the New Jerusalem,
And held your trailing lutestring up yourself

From brushing the twelve stones, for fear of some
Small speck as little as a needle-prick,
White stitched on white, — the child would keep to
    me,
Would choose his poor lost Marian, like me best,
And, though you stretched your arms, cry back and
    cling,
As we do when God says it's time to die   720
And bids us go up higher.   Leave us, then ;
We two are happy.   Does *he* push me off?
He's satisfied with me, as I with him.''

"So soft to one, so hard to others !   Nay,"
I cried, more angry that she melted me,
" We make henceforth a cushion of our faults
To sit and practise easy virtues on ?
I thought a child was given to sanctify
A woman, — set her in the sight of all
The clear-eyed heavens, a chosen minister   730
To do their business and lead spirits up
The difficult blue heights.   A woman lives,
Not bettered, quickened toward the truth and good
Through being a mother ? . . . then she's none !
    although
She damps her baby's cheeks by kissing them,
As we kill roses."
            " Kill ! O Christ,'' she said,
And turned her wild sad face from side to side
With most despairing wonder in it, " What,
What have you in your souls against me then,
All of you ? am I wicked, do you think ?   740
God knows me, trusts me with the child ; but you,
You think me really wicked ? ''
                  " Complaisant,''

I answered softly, " to a wrong you've done,
Because of certain profits, — which is wrong
Beyond the first wrong, Marian.   When you left
The pure place and the noble heart, to take
The hand of a seducer "   .   .   .
                    " Whom ? whose hand ?
I took the hand of "   .   .   .
                        Springing up erect,
And lifting up the child at full arm's length,
As if to bear him like an oriflamme   750
Unconquerable to armies of reproach, —
" By *him*," she said, " my child's head and its curls,
By these blue eyes no woman born could dare
A perjury on, I make my mother's oath,
That if I left that Heart, to lighten it,
The blood of mine was still, except for grief !
No cleaner maid than I was took a step
To a sadder end, — no matron-mother now
Looks backward to her early maidenhood
Through chaster pulses.   I speak steadily ;   760
And if I lie so,   .   .   if, being fouled in will
And paltered with in soul by devil's lust,
I dared to bid this angel take my part,   .   .   .
Would God sit quiet, let us think, in heaven,
Nor strike me dumb with thunder ?   Yet I speak :
He clears me therefore.   What, ' seduced ' 's your
        word !
Do wolves seduce a wandering fawn in France ?
Do eagles, who have pinched a lamb with claws,
Seduce it into carrion ?   So with me.
I was not ever, as you say, seduced,   770
But simply, murdered."
                        There she paused, and sighed
With such a sigh as drops from agony

To exhaustion, — sighing while she let the babe
Slide down upon her bosom from her arms,
And all her face's light fell after him
Like a torch quenched in falling.   Down she sank,
And sat upon the bedside with the child.

But I, convicted, broken utterly,
With woman's passion clung about her waist   779
And kissed her hair and eyes, — " I have been wrong,
Sweet   Marian "   .   .   .   (weeping   in   a   tender
     rage) . . .
" Sweet holy Marian !   And now, Marian, now,
I'll use your oath although my lips are hard,
And by the child, my Marian, by the child,
l swear his mother shall be innocent
Before my conscience, as in the open Book
Of Him who reads for judgment.   Innocent,
My sister ! let the night be ne'er so dark
The moon is surely somewhere in the sky ;
So surely is your whiteness to be found   790
Through all dark facts.   But pardon, pardon me,
And smile a little, Marian, — for the child,
If not for me, my sister."
                              The poor lip
Just motioned for the smile and let it go :
And then, with scarce a stirring of the mouth,
As if a statue spoke that could not breathe,
But spoke on calm between its marble lips, —
" I'm glad, I'm very glad you clear me so.
I should be sorry that you set me down
With harlots, or with even a better name   800
Which misbecomes his mother.   For the rest,
I am not on a level with your love,
Nor ever was, you know, — but now am worse,

Because that world of yours has dealt with me
As when the hard sea bites and chews a stone
And changes the first form of it.   I've marked
A shore of pebbles bitten to one shape
From all the various life of madrepores ;
And so, that little stone, called Marian Erle,   809
Picked up and dropped by you and another friend,
Was ground and tortured by the incessant sea
And bruised from what she was, — changed ! death's
    a change,
And she, I said, was murdered ; Marian's dead.
What can you do with people when they are dead
But, if you are pious, sing a hymn and go ;
Or, if you are tender, heave a sigh and go ;
But go by all means, — and permit the grass
To keep its green feud up 'twixt them and you ?
Then leave me, — let me rest.   I'm dead, I say,
And if, to save the child from death as well,   820
The mother in me has survived the rest,
Why, that's God's miracle you must not tax,
I'm not less dead for that . I'm nothing more
But just a mother.   Only for the child
I'm warm, and cold, and hungry, and afraid,
And smell the flowers a little and see the sun,
And speak still, and am silent, — just for him !
I pray you therefore to mistake me not
And treat me haply as I were alive ;
For though you ran a pin into my soul,   830
I think it would not hurt nor trouble me.
Here's proof, dear lady, — in the market-place
But now, you promised me to say a word
About . . . a friend, who once, long years ago,
Took God's place toward me, when He leans and
    loves

And does not thunder, . . . whom at last I left,
As all of us leave God.　You thought perhaps
I seemed to care for hearing of that friend ?
Now, judge me ! we have sat here half an hour
And talked together of the child and me,　　840
And I not asked as much as ' What's the thing
' You had to tell me of the friend . . . the friend ? '
He's sad, I think you said, — he's sick perhaps ?
'Tis nought to Marian if he's sad or sick.
Another would have crawled beside your foot
And prayed your words out.　Why, a beast, a dog,
A starved cat, if he had fed it once with milk,
Would show less hardness.　But I'm dead, you see,
And that explains it.''

　　　　　　　　Poor, poor thing, she spoke
And shook her head, as white and calm as frost　850
On days too cold for raining any more,
But still with such a face, so much alive,
I could not choose but take it on my arm
And stroke the placid patience of its cheeks, —
Then told my story out, of Romney Leigh,
How, having lost her, sought her, missed her still,
He, broken-hearted for himself and her,
Had drawn the curtains of the world awhile　858
As if he had done with morning.　There I stopped,
For when she gasped, and pressed me with her eyes,
'' And now . . . how is it with him ? tell me
　　now,''
I felt the shame of compensated grief,
And chose my words with scruple — slowly stepped
Upon the slippery stones set here and there
Across the sliding water.　'' Certainly,
As evening empties morning into night,
Another morning takes the evening up

With healthful, providential interchange ;
And, though he thought still of her —— ''
                                        '' Yes, she knew,
She understood : she had supposed indeed   870
That, as one stops a hole upon a flute,
At which a new note comes and shapes the tune,
Excluding her would bring a worthier in,
And, long ere this, that Lady Waldemar
He loved so '' . . .
                '' Loved,'' I started, — '' loved her so !
Now tell me '' . . .
                        '' I will tell you,'' she replied :
'' But, since we're taking oaths, you'll promise first
That he in England, he, shall never learn
In what a dreadful trap his creature here,
Round whose unworthy neck he had meant to tie 880
The honourable ribbon of his name,
Fell unaware and came to butchery :
Because, — I know him, — as he takes to heart
The grief of every stranger, he's not like
To banish mine as far as I should choose
In wishing him most happy.   Now he leaves
To think of me, perverse, who went my way,
Unkind, and left him, — but if once he knew . . .
Ah, then, the sharp nail of my cruel wrong
Would fasten me forever in his sight,   890
Like some poor curious bird, through each spread
        wing
Nailed high up over a fierce hunter's fire,
To spoil the dinner of all tenderer folk
Come in by chance.   Nay, since your Marian's dead,
You shall not hang her up, but dig a hole
And bury her in silence ! ring no bells.''

I answered gaily, though my whole voice wept,
" We'll ring the joy-bells, not the funeral-bells,
Because we have her back, dead or alive."

She never answered that, but shook her head ;   900
Then low and calm, as one who, safe in heaven,
Shall tell a story of his lower life,
Unmoved by shame or anger, — so she spoke.
She told me she had loved upon her knees,
As others pray, more perfectly absorbed
In the act and inspiration.   She felt his
For just his uses, not her own at all, —
His stool, to sit on or put up his foot,
His cup, to fill with wine or vinegar,
Whichever drink might please him at the chance, 910
For that should please her always : let him write
His name upon her . . . it seemed natural ;
It was most precious, standing on his shelf,
To wait until he chose to lift his hand.
Well, well, — I saw her then, and must have seen
How bright her life went floating on her love,
Like wicks the housewives send afloat on oil
Which feeds them to a flame that lasts the night.

To do good seemed so much his business,
That, having done it, she was fain to think,   920
Must fill up his capacity for joy.
At first she never mooted with herself
If *he* was happy, since he made her so,
Or if he loved her, being so much beloved.
Who thinks of asking if the sun is light,
Observing that it lightens ? who's so bold
To question God of His felicity ?
Still less.   And thus she took for granted first

What first of all she should have put to proof,
And sinned against him so, but only so.   930
" What could you hope," she said, " of such as she ?
You take a kid you like, and turn it out
In some fair garden : though the creature's fond
And gentle, it will leap upon the beds
And break your tulips, bite your tender trees ;
The wonder would be if such innocence
Spoiled less : a garden is no place for kids."
And, by degrees, when he who had chosen her
Brought in his courteous and benignant friends
To spend their goodness on her, which she took   940
So very gladly, as a part of his, —
By slow degrees it broke on her slow sense
That she too in that Eden of delight
Was out of place, and, like the silly kid,
Still did most mischief where she meant most love.
A thought enough to make a woman mad
(No beast in this but she may well go mad),
That saying " I am thine to love and use "
May blow the plague in her protesting breath
To the very man for whom she claims to die, — 950
That, clinging round his neck, she pulls him down
And drowns him, — and that, lavishing her soul,
She hales perdition on him.   " So, being mad,"
Said Marian . . .

           " Ah — who stirred such thoughts, you ask ?
Whose fault it was, that she should have such
     thoughts ?
None's fault, none's fault.   The light comes, and we
     see :
But if it were not truly for our eyes,
There would be nothing seen, for all the light.
And so with Marian : if she saw at last,

The sense was in her, — Lady Waldemar   960
Had spoken all in vain else.''

                              '' O my heart,
O prophet in my heart,'' I cried aloud,
'' Then Lady Waldemar spoke ! ''

                              '' *Did* she speak,''
Mused Marian softly, '' or did she only sign ?
Or did she put a word into her face
And look, and so impress you with the word ?
Or leave it in the foldings of her gown,
Like rosemary smells a movement will shake out
When no one's conscious ? who shall say, or guess ?
One thing alone was certain — from the day   970
The gracious lady paid a visit first,
She, Marian, saw things different, — felt distrust
Of all that sheltering roof of circumstance
Her hopes were building into the clay nests :
Her heart was restless, pacing up and down
And fluttering, like dumb creatures before storms,
Not knowing wherefore she was ill at ease.''

'' And still the lady came,'' said Marian Erle,
'' Much oftener than *he* knew it, Mister Leigh.
She bade me never tell him she had come,   980
She liked to love me better than he knew,
So very kind was Lady Waldemar :
And every time she brought with her more light,
And every light made sorrow clearer . . . Well,
Ah, well ! we cannot give her blame for that ;
'Twould be the same thing if an angel came,
Whose right should prove our wrong. And every
          time
The lady came, she looked more beautiful
And spoke more like a flute among green trees,

Until at last, as one, whose heart being sad   990
On hearing lovely music, suddenly
Dissolves in weeping, I brake out in tears
Before her, asked her counsel, — 'Had I erred
'In being too happy? would she set me straight?
'For she, being wise and good and born above
'The flats I had never climbed from, could perceive
'If such as I might grow upon the hills;
'And whether such poor herb sufficed to grow,
'For Romney Leigh to break his fast upon't, —
'Or would he pine on such, or haply starve?'   1000
She wrapped me in her generous arms at once,
And let me dream a moment how it feels
To have a real mother, like some girls:
But when I looked, her face was younger . . . ay,
Youth's too bright not to be a little hard,
And beauty keeps itself still uppermost,
That's true! — Though Lady Waldemar was kind
She hurt me, hurt, as if the morning sun
Should smite us on the eyelids when we sleep,
And wake us up with headache.   Ay, and soon   1010
Was light enough to make my heart ache too:
She told me truths I asked for, — 'twas my fault, —
'That Romney could not love me, if he would,
'As men call loving: there are bloods that flow
'Together like some rivers and not mix,
'Through contraries of nature.   He indeed
'Was set to wed me, to espouse my class,
'Act out a rash opinion, — and, once wed,
'So just a man and gentle could not choose
'But make my life as smooth as marriage-ring,   1020
'Bespeak me mildly, keep me a cheerful house,
'With servants, brooches, all the flowers I liked,
'And pretty dresses, silk the whole year round' . . .

At which I stopped her, — ' This for me.   And now
' For *him*.' — She hesitated, — truth grew hard ;
She owned ' 'Twas plain a man like Romney Leigh
' Required a wife more level to himself.
' If day by day he had to bend his height
' To pick up sympathies, opinions, thoughts,
' And interchange the common talk of life   1030
' Which helps a man to live as well as talk,
' His days were heavily taxed.   Who buys a staff
' To fit the hand, that reaches but the knee ?
' He'd feel it bitter to be forced to miss
' The perfect joy of married suited pairs,
' Who, bursting through the separating hedge
' Of personal dues with that sweet eglantine
' Of equal love, keep saying, " So *we* think,
' " It strikes *us*, — that's *our* fancy." ' — When I
        asked
If earnest will, devoted love, employed   1040
In youth like mine, would fail to raise me up
As two strong arms will always raise a child
To a fruit hung overhead, she sighed and sighed . . .
' That could not be,' she feared.   ' You take a pink,
' You dig about its roots and water it
' And so improve it to a garden-pink,
' But will not change it to a heliotrope,
' The kind remains.   And then, the harder truth —
' This Romney Leigh, so rash to leap a pale,
' So bold for conscience, quick for martyrdom,   1050
' Would suffer steadily and never flinch,
' But suffer surely and keenly, when his class
' Turned shoulder on him for a shameful match,
' And set him up as nine-pin in their talk
' To bowl him down with jestings.' — There, she
        paused.

And when I used the pause in doubting that
We wronged him after all in what we feared —
' Suppose such things could never touch him more
' In his high conscience (if the things should be)
' Than, when the queen sits in an upper room,　1060
' The horses in the street can spatter her ! ' —
A moment, hope came, — but the lady closed
That door and nicked the lock and shut it out,
Observing wisely that ' the tender heart
' Which made him over-soft to a lower class,
' Would scarcely fail to make him sensitive
' To a higher, — how they thought and what they
　　felt.'

" Alas, alas ! " said Marian, rocking slow
The pretty baby who was near asleep,
The eyelids creeping over the blue balls, —　1070
" She made it clear, too clear — I saw the whole !
And yet who knows if I had seen my way
Straight out of it by looking, though 'twas clear,
Unless the generous lady, 'ware of this,
Had set her own house all a-fire for me
To light me forwards ?　Leaning on my face
Her heavy agate eyes which crushed my will,
She told me tenderly (as when men come
To a bedside to tell people they must die),　1079
' She knew of knowledge, — ay, of knowledge knew,
' That Romney Leigh had loved *her* formerly.
' And *she* loved *him*, she might say, now the chance
' Was passed,— but that, of course, he never guessed,—
' For something came between them, something thin
' As a cobweb, catching every fly of doubt
' To hold it buzzing at the window-pane
' And help to dim the daylight.　Ah, man's pride

' Or woman's — which is greatest ? most averse
' To brushing cobwebs ?   Well, but she and he   1089
' Remained fast friends ; it seemed not more than so,
' Because he had bound his hands and could not stir.
' An honourable man, if somewhat rash ;
' And she, not even for Romney, would she spill
' A blot . . . as little even as a tear . . .
' Upon his marriage-contract, — not to gain
' A better joy for two than came by that :
' For, though I stood between her heart and heaven,
' She loved me wholly.' "

       Did I laugh or curse ?
I think I sat there silent, hearing all,
Ay, hearing double, — Marian's tale, at once,   1100
And Romney's marriage vow " *I'll keep to* THEE,"
Which means that woman-serpent.   Is it time
For church now ?

      " Lady Waldemar spoke more,"
Continued Marian, "but, as when a soul
Will pass out through the sweetness of a song
Beyond it, voyaging the uphill road,
Even so mine wandered from the things I heard
To those I suffered.   It was afterward
I shaped the resolution to the act.   1109
For many hours we talked.   What need to talk ?
The fate was clear and close ; it touched my eyes ;
But still the generous lady tried to keep
The case afloat, and would not let it go,
And argued, struggled upon Marian's side,
Which was not Romney's ! though she little knew
What ugly monster would take up the end, —
What griping death within the drowning death
Was ready to complete my sum of death."

I thought, — Perhaps he's sliding now the ring 1119
Upon that woman's finger . . .

      She went on :

"The lady, failing to prevail her way,
Upgathered my torn wishes from the ground
And pieced them with her strong benevolence ;
And, as I thought I could breathe freer air
Away from England, going without pause,
Without farewell, just breaking with a jerk
The blossomed offshoot from my thorny life, —
She promised kindly to provide the means,
With instant passage to the colonies   1129
And full protection, — ' would commit me straight
'To one who once had been her waiting-maid
' And had the customs of the world, intent
' On changing England for Australia
' Herself, to carry out her fortune so.'
For which I thanked the Lady Waldemar,
As men upon their death-beds thank last friends
Who lay the pillow straight : it is not much,
And yet 'tis all of which they are capable,
This lying smoothly in a bed to die.   1139
And so, 'twas fixed ; — and so, from day to day,
The woman named came in to visit me."

Just then the girl stopped speaking, — sat erect,
And stared at me as if I had been a ghost
(Perhaps I looked as white as any ghost),
With large-eyed horror. "Does God make," she
    said,
" All sorts of creatures really, do you think ?
Or is it that the Devil slavers them
So excellently, that we come to doubt
Who's stronger, He who makes, or he who mars ?

I never liked the woman's face or voice   1150
Or ways : it made me blush to look at her ;
It made me tremble if she touched my hand ;
And when she spoke a fondling word I shrank
As if one hated me who had power to hurt ;
And, every time she came, my veins ran cold
As somebody were walking on my grave.
At last I spoke to Lady Waldemar :
' Could such an one be good to trust ? ' I asked.
Whereat the lady stroked my cheek and laughed
Her silver-laugh (one must be born to laugh,   1160
To put such music in it), — ' Foolish girl,
' Your scattered wits are gathering wool beyond
' The sheep-walk reaches ! — leave the thing to me.'
And therefore, half in trust, and half in scorn
That I had heart still for another fear
In such a safe despair, I left the thing.

" The rest is short.   I was obedient :
I wrote my letter which delivered *him*
From Marian to his own prosperities,   1169
And followed that bad guide.   The lady ? — hush,
I never blame the lady.   Ladies who
Sit high, however willing to look down,
Will scarce see lower than their dainty feet ;
And Lady Waldemar saw less than I
With what a Devil's daughter I went forth
Along the swine's road, down the precipice,
In such a curl of hell-foam caught and choked,
No shriek of soul in anguish could pierce through
To fetch some help.   They say there's help in
          heaven   1179
For all such cries.   But if one cries from hell . . .
What then ? — the heavens are deaf upon that side.

" A woman . . . hear me, let me make it plain, . . .
A woman . . . not a monster . . . both her
    breasts
Made right to suckle babes . . . she took me off
A woman also, young and ignorant
And heavy with my grief, my two poor eyes
Near washed away with weeping, till the trees,
The blessed unaccustomed trees and fields
Ran either side the train like stranger dogs
Unworthy of any notice, — took me off   1190
So dull, so blind, so only half-alive,
Not seeing by what road, nor by what ship,
Nor toward what place, nor to what end of all.
Men carry a corpse thus, — past the doorway, past
The garden-gate, the children's playground, up
The green lane, — then they leave it in the pit,
To sleep and find corruption, cheek to cheek
With him who stinks since Friday.

                  " But suppose ;
To go down with one's soul into the grave,
To go down half-dead, half alive, I say,   1200
And wake up with corruption, . . . cheek to cheek
With him who stinks since Friday ! There it is,
And that's the horror of't, Miss Leigh.

                 " You feel ?
You understand ? — no, do not look at me,
But understand.   The blank, blind, weary way,
Which led, where'er it led, away at least ;
The shifted ship, to Sydney or to France,
Still bound, wherever else, to another land ;
The swooning sickness on the dismal sea,   1209
The foreign shore, the shameful house, the night,
The feeble blood, the heavy-headed grief, . . .
No need to bring their damnable drugged cup,

And yet they brought it.   Hell's so prodigal
Of devil's gifts, hunts liberally in packs,
Will kill no poor small creature of the wilds
But fifty red wide throats must smoke at it,
As HIS at me . . . when waking up his last . . .
I told you that I waked up in the grave.

" Enough so ! — it is plain enough so.   True,
We wretches cannot tell out all our wrong   1220
Without offence to decent happy folk.
I know that we must scrupulously hint
With half-words, delicate reserves, the thing
Which no one scrupled we should feel in full.
Let pass the rest, then ; only leave my oath
Upon this sleeping child, — man's violence,
Not man's seduction, made me what I am,
As lost as . . . I told *him* I should be lost.
When mothers fail us, can we help ourselves ?
That's fatal ! — And you call it being lost,   1230
That down came next day's noon and caught me
    there,
Half-gibbering and half-raving on the floor,
And wondering what had happened up in heaven,
That suns should dare to shine when God Himself
Was certainly abolished.

                " I was mad,
How many weeks, I know not, — many weeks.
I think they let me go when I was mad,
They feared my eyes and loosed me, as boys might
A mad dog which they had tortured.   Up and down
I went, by road and village, over tracts   1240
Of open foreign country, large and strange,
Crossed everywhere by long thin poplar-lines
Like fingers of some ghastly skeleton Hand

Through sunlight and through moonlight evermore
Pushed out from hell itself to pluck me back,
And resolute to get me, slow and sure ;
While every roadside Christ upon his cross
Hung reddening through his gory wounds at me,
And shook his nails in anger, and came down
To follow a mile after, wading up   1250
The low vines and green wheat, crying ' Take the
     girl !
' She's none of mine from henceforth.' Then I
     knew
(But this is somewhat dimmer than the rest)
The charitable peasants gave me bread
And leave to sleep in straw : and twice they tied,
At parting, Mary's image round my neck —
How heavy it seemed ! as heavy as a stone ;
A woman has been strangled with less weight :
I threw it in a ditch to keep it clean   1259
And ease my breath a little, when none looked ;
I did not need such safeguards : — brutal men
Stopped short. Miss Leigh, in insult, when they had
     seen
My face, — I must have had an awful look.
And so I lived : the weeks passed on, — I lived.
'Twas living my old tramp-life o'er again,
But, this time, in a dream, and hunted round
By some prodigious Dream-fear at my back,
Which ended yet : my brain cleared presently ;
And there I sat, one evening, by the road,
I, Marian Erle, myself, alone, undone,   1270
Facing a sunset low upon the flats
As if it were the finish of all time,
The great red stone upon my sepulchre,
Which angels were too weak to roll away.

SEVENTH BOOK.

" THE woman's motive ? shall we daub ourselves
With finding roots for nettles ? 'tis soft clay
And easily explored.   She had the means,
The moneys, by the lady's liberal grace,
In trust for that Australian scheme and me,
Which so, that she might clutch with both her hands
And chink to her naughty uses undisturbed,
She served me (after all it was not strange,
'Twas only what my mother would have done)
A motherly, right damnable good turn.   10

" Well, after.   There are nettles everywhere,
But smooth green grasses are more common still ;
The blue of heaven is larger than the cloud ;
A miller's wife at Clichy took me in
And spent her pity on me, — made me calm
And merely very reasonably sad.
She found me a servant's place in Paris, where
I tried to take the cast-off life again,
And stood as quiet as a beaten ass
Who, having fallen through overloads, stands up   20
To let them charge him with another pack.

" A   few   months, so.   My mistress, young and
    light,
Was easy with me, less for kindness than
Because she led, herself, an easy time
Betwixt her lover and her looking-glass,
Scarce knowing which way she was praised the most.
She felt so pretty and so pleased all day
She could not take the trouble to be cross,
But sometimes, as I stooped to tie her shoe,

Would tap me softly with her slender foot   30
Still restless with the last night's dancing in't,
And say ' Fie, pale-face ! are you English girls
' All grave and silent ? mass-book still, and Lent ?
' And first-communion pallor on your cheeks,
' Worn past the time for't ? little fool, be gay ! '
At which she vanished like a fairy, through
A gap of silver laughter.
                    " Came an hour
When all went otherwise.   She did not speak,
But clenched her brows, and clipped me with her
    eyes
As if a viper with a pair of tongs,   40
Too far for any touch, yet near enough
To view the writhing creature, — then at last,
' Stand still there, in the holy Virgin's name,
' Thou Marian ; thou'rt no reputable girl,
' Although sufficient dull for twenty saints !
' I think thou mock'st me and my house,' she said ;
' Confess thou'lt be a mother in a month,
' Thou mask of saintship.'
                   " Could I answer her ?
The light broke in so.   It meant *that* then, *that ?*
I had not thought of that, in all my thoughts,   50
Through all the cold, numb aching of my brow,
Through all the heaving of impatient life
Which threw me on death at intervals, — through
    all
The upbreak of the fountain of my heart
The rains had swelled too large : it could mean *that ?*
Did God make mothers out of victims, then,
And set such pure amens to hideous deeds ?
Why not ? He overblows an ugly grave
With violets which blossom in the spring.

And *I* could be a mother in a month ?   60
I hope it was not wicked to be glad.
I lifted up my voice and wept, and laughed,
To heaven, not her, until it tore my throat.
' Confess, confess ! ' — what was there to confess,
Except man's cruelty, except my wrong ?
Except this anguish, or this ecstasy ?
This shame or glory ? The light woman there
Was small to take it in : an acorn-cup
Would take the sea in sooner.

                          " ' Good,' she cried ;
" Unmarried and a mother, and she laughs !   70
' These unchaste girls are always impudent.
' Get out, intriguer ! leave my house and trot.
' I wonder you should look me in the face,
' With such a filthy secret.'

                     "Then I rolled
My scanty bundle up and went my way,
Washed white with weeping, shuddering head and
    foot
With blind hysteric passion, staggering forth
Beyond those doors.   'Twas natural of course
She should not ask me where I meant to sleep ;
I might sleep well beneath the heavy Seine,   80
Like others of my sort ; the bed was laid
For us.   But any woman, womanly,
Had thought of him who should be in a month,
The sinless babe that should be in a month,
And if by chance he might be warmer housed
Than underneath such dreary dripping eaves.''

I broke on Marian there.   '' Yet she herself,
A wife, I think, had scandals of her own, —
A lover not her husband.''

                     " Ay," she said,
" But gold and meal are measured otherwise ;   90
I learnt so much at school," said Marian Erle.

" O crooked world," I cried, " ridiculous
If not so lamentable !   'Tis the way
With these light women of a thrifty vice,
My Marian, — always hard upon the rent
In any sister's virtue ! while they keep
Their own so darned and patched with perfidy,
That, though a rag itself, it looks as well
Across a street, in balcony or coach,
As any perfect stuff might.   For my part,   100
I'd rather take the wind-side of the stews
Than touch such women with my finger-end !
They top the poor street-walker by their lie
And look the better for being so much worse :
The devil's most devilish when respectable.
But you, dear, and your story."
                         " All the rest
Is here," she said, and signed upon the child.
" I found a mistress-sempstress who was kind
And let me sew in peace among her girls.
And what was better than to draw the threads   110
All day and half the night for him and him ?
And so I lived for him, and so he lives,
And so I know, by this time, God lives too."

She smiled beyond the sun and ended so,
And all my soul rose up to take her part
Against the world's successes, virtues, fames.
" Come with me, sweetest sister," I returned,
" And sit within my house and do me good
From henceforth, thou and thine ! ye are my own

From henceforth.   I am lonely in the world,   120
And thou art lonely, and the child is half
An orphan.   Come,— and henceforth thou and I
Being still together will not miss a friend,
Nor he a father, since two mothers shall
Make that up to him.   I am journeying south,
And in my Tuscan home I'll find a niche
And set thee there, my saint, the child and thee,
And burn the lights of love before thy face,
And ever at thy sweet look cross myself
From mixing with the world's prosperities ;   130
That so, in gravity and holy calm,
We two may live on toward the truer life."

She looked me in the face and answered not,
Nor signed she was unworthy, nor gave thanks,
But took the sleeping child and held it out
To meet my kiss, as if requiting me
And trusting me at once.   And thus, at once,
I carried him and her to where I live ;
She's there now, in the little room, asleep,
I hear the soft child-breathing through the door,   140
And all three of us, at to-morrow's break,
Pass onward, homeward, to our Italy.
Oh, Romney Leigh, I have your debts to pay,
And I'll be just and pay them.
                                          But yourself !
To pay your debts is scarcely difficult,
To buy your life is nearly impossible,
Being sold away to Lamia.   My head aches,
I cannot see my road along this dark ;
Nor can I creep and grope, as fits the dark,
For these foot-catching robes of womanhood :   150
A man might walk a little . . . but I ! — He loves

The Lamia-woman,— and I, write to him
What stops his marriage, and destroys his peace,—
Or what perhaps shall simply trouble him,
Until she only need to touch his sleeve
With just a finger's tremulous white flame,
Saying " Ah,— Aurora Leigh ! a pretty tale,
" A very pretty poet !   I can guess
" The motive " — then, to catch his eye in hers
And vow she does not wonder, — and they two   160
To break in laughter as the sea along
A melancholy coast, and float up higher,
In such a laugh, their fatal weeds of love !
Ay, fatal, ay.   And who shall answer me
Fate has not hurried tides, — and if to-night
My letter would not be a night too late,
An arrow shot into a man that's dead,
To prove a vain intention ?   Would I show
The new wife vile, to make the husband mad ?
No, Lamia ! shut the shutters, bar the doors   170
From every glimmer on thy serpent-skin !
I will not let thy hideous secret out
To agonize the man I love — I mean
The friend I love . . . as friends love.

                            It is strange,
To-day while Marian told her story like
To absorb most listeners, how I listened chief
To a voice not hers, nor yet that enemy's,
Nor God's in wrath, . . . but one that mixed
    with mine
Long years ago among the garden-trees,
And said to *me*, to *me* too, " Be my wife,   180
Aurora."   It is strange with what a swell
Of yearning passion, as a snow of ghosts
Might beat against the impervious door of heaven,

I thought, " Now, if I had been a woman, such
As God made women, to save men by love, —
By just my love I might have saved this man,
And made a nobler poem for the world
Than all I have failed in." 　But I failed besides
In this ; and now he's lost ! through me alone !
And, by my only fault, his empty house　　　190
Sucks in, at this same hour, a wind from hell
To keep his hearth cold, make his casements creak
For ever to the tune of plague and sin —
O Romney, O my Romney, O my friend,
My cousin and friend ! my helper, when I would,
My love, that might be ! mine !
　　　　　　　　　　　　　Why, how one weeps
When one's too weary ! 　Were a witness by,
He'd say some folly . . . that I love the man,
Who knows ? . . . and make me laugh again for
　　　scorn.
At strongest, women are as weak in flesh,　　200
As men, at weakest, vilest, are in soul :
So, hard for women to keep pace with men !
As well give up at once, sit down at once,
And weep as I do. 　Tears, tears ! *why* we weep ?
'Tis worth inquiry ? — that we've shamed a life,
Or lost a love, or missed a world, perhaps ?
By no means. 　Simply, that we've walked too far,
Or talked too much, or felt the wind i' the east, —
And so we weep, as if both body and soul
Broke up in water — this way.
　　　　　　　　　　　Poor mixed rags　210
Forsooth we're made of, like those other dolls
That lean with pretty faces into fairs.
It seems as if I had a man in me,
Despising such a woman.

                                Yet indeed,
To see a wrong or suffering moves us all
To undo it though we should undo ourselves,
Ay, all the more, that we undo ourselves ;
That's womanly, past doubt, and not ill-moved.
A natural movement therefore, on my part,
To fill the chair up of my cousin's wife,   220
And save him from a devil's company !
We're all so, — made so — 'tis our woman's trade
To suffer torment for another's ease.
The world's male chivalry has perished out,
But women are knights-errant to the last ;
And if Cervantes had been Shakespeare too,
He had made his Don a Donna.

                                    So it clears,
And so we rain our skies blue.

                                Put away
This weakness.   If, as I have just now said,
A man's within me, — let him act himself,   230
Ignoring the poor conscious trouble of blood
That's called the woman merely.   I will write
Plain words to England, — if too late, too late,
If ill-accounted, then accounted ill ;
We'll trust the heavens with something.

                                " Dear Lord Howe,
You'll find a story on another leaf
Of Marian Erle, — what noble friend of yours
She trusted once, through what flagitious means,
To what disastrous ends ; — the story's true.
I found her wandering on the Paris quays,   240
A babe upon her breast, — unnatural,
Unseasonable outcast on such snow
Unthawed to this time.   I will tax in this
Your friendship, friend, if that convicted She

Be not his wife yet, to denounce the facts
To himself, — but, otherwise, to let them pass
On tip-toe like escaping murderers,
And tell my cousin merely — Marian lives,
Is found, and finds her home with such a friend, 249
Myself, Aurora.   Which good news, 'She's found,'
Will help to make him merry in his love·:
I send it, tell him, for my marriage-gift,
As good as orange water for the nerves,
Or perfumed gloves for headache, — though aware
That he, except of love, is scarcely sick :
I mean the new love this time, . . . since last
      year.
Such quick forgetting on the part of men !
Is any shrewder trick upon the cards
To enrich them ? pray instruct me how 'tis done :
First, clubs, — and while you look at clubs, 'tis
      spades ;   260
That prodigy.   The lightning strikes a man,
And when we think to find him dead and charred . . .
Why, there he is on a sudden, playing pipes
Beneath the splintered elm-tree !   Crime and shame
And all their hoggery trample your smooth world,
Nor leave more foot-marks than Apollo's kine
Whose hoofs were muffled by the thieving god
In tamarisk-leaves and myrtle.   I'm so sad,
So weary and sad to-night, I'm somewhat sour, —
Forgive me.   To be blue and shrew at once   270
Exceeds all toleration except yours,
But yours, I know, is infinite.   Farewell.
To-morrow we take train for Italy.
Speak gently of me to your gracious wife,
As one, however far, shall yet be
In loving wishes to your house.'' near

I sign.
And now I loose my heart upon a page,
This —

      " Lady Waldemar, I'm very glad
I never liked you ; which you knew so well
You spared me, in your turn, to like me much :   280
Your liking surely had done worse for me
Than has your loathing, though the last appears
Sufficiently unscrupulous to hurt,
And not afraid of judgment.   Now, there's space
Between our faces, — I stand off, as if
I judged a stranger's portrait and pronounced
Indifferently the type was good or bad.
What matter to me that the lines are false,
I ask you ? did I ever ink my lips
By drawing your name through them as a friend's,   290
Or touch your hand as lovers do ?   Thank God
I never did : and since you're proved so vile,
Ay, vile, I say, — we'll show it presently, —
I'm not obliged to nurse my friend in you,
Or wash out my own blots, in counting yours,
Or even excuse myself to honest souls
Who seek to press my lip or clasp my palm, —
' Alas, but Lady Waldemar came first ! '

    " 'Tis true, by this time you may near me so   299
That you're my cousin's wife.   You've gambled deep
As Lucifer, and won the morning-star
In that case, — and the noble house of Leigh
Must henceforth with its good roof shelter you :
I cannot speak and burn you up between
Those rafters, I who am born a Leigh, — nor speak
And pierce your breast through Romney's, I who live,
His friend and cousin, — so, you're safe.   You two

Must grow together like the tares and wheat
Till God's great fire. — But make the best of time.

"And hide this letter: let it speak no more   310
Than I shall, how you tricked poor Marian Erle,
And set her own love digging its own grave
Within her green hope's pretty garden-ground, —
Ay, sent her forth with some one of your sort
To a wicked house in France, from which she fled
With curses in her eyes and ears and throat,
Her whole soul choked with curses, — mad in short,
And madly scouring up and down for weeks
The foreign hedgeless country, lone and lost, —
So innocent, male-fiends might slink within   320
Remote hell-corners, seeing her so defiled.

"But you, — you are a woman and more bold.
To do you justice, you'd not shrink to face . . .
We'll say, the unfledged life in the other room,
Which, treading down God's corn, you trod in sight
Of all the dogs, in reach of all the guns, —
Ay, Marian's babe, her poor unfathered child,
Her yearling babe! — you'd face him when he wakes
And opens up his wonderful blue eyes:
You'd meet them and not wink perhaps, nor fear 330
God's triumph in them and supreme revenge
When righting His creation's balance-scale
(You pulled as low as Tophet) to the top
Of most celestial innocence.   For me,
Who am not as bold, I own those infant eyes
Have set me praying.

                              "While they look at heaven,
No need of protestation in my words
Against the place you've made them! let them look.

They'll do your business with the heavens, be sure :
I spare you common curses.

                      " Ponder this ;   340
If haply you're the wife of Romney Leigh
(For which inheritance beyond your birth
You sold that poisonous porridge called your soul),
I charge you, be his faithful and true wife !
Keep warm his hearth and clean his board, and, when
He speaks, be quick with your obedience ;
Still grind your paltry wants and low desires
To dust beneath his heel ; though, even thus,
The ground must hurt him, — it was writ of old,
' Ye shall not yoke together ox and ass,'   350
The nobler and ignobler.   Ay, but you
Shall do your part as well as such ill things
Can do aught good.   You shall not vex him, — mark,
You shall not vex him, jar him when he's sad,
Or cross him when he's eager.   Understand
To trick him with apparent sympathies,
Nor let him see thee in the face too near
And unlearn thy sweet seeming.   Pay the price
Of lies, by being constrained to lie on still :
'Tis easy for thy sort : a million more   360
Will scarcely damn thee deeper.

                          " Doing which
You are very safe from Marian and myself ;
We'll breathe as softly as the infant here,
And stir no dangerous embers.   Fail a point,
And show our Romney wounded, ill-content,
Tormented in his home, we open mouth,
And such a noise will follow, the last trump's
Will scarcely seem more dreadful, even to you ;
You'll have no pipers after : Romney will
(I know him) push you forth as none of his,   370

All other men declaring it well done,
While women, even the worst, your like, will draw
Their skirts back, not to brush you in the street,
And so I warn you. I'm . . . Aurora Leigh."

The letter written, I felt satisfied.
The ashes, smouldering in me, were thrown out
By handfuls from me : I had writ my heart
And wept my tears, and now was cool and calm ;
And, going straightway to the neighbouring room,
I lifted up the curtains of the bed　　　　　380
Where Marian Erle, the babe upon her arm,
Both faces leaned together like a pair
Of folded innocences self-complete,
Each smiling from the other, smiled and slept.
There seemed no sin, no shame, no wrath, no grief.
I felt she too had spoken words that night,
But softer certainly, and said to God,
Who laughs in heaven perhaps that such as I
Should make ado for such as she. — " Defiled "
I wrote ? " defiled " I thought her ?　Stoop,　390
Stoop lower, Aurora ! get the angels' leave
To creep in somewhere, humbly, on your knees,
Within this round of sequestration white
In which they have wrapped earth's foundlings, heaven's
　　　elect.

The next day we took train to Italy
And fled on southward in the roar of steam.
The marriage bells of Romney must be loud,
To sound so clear through all : I was not well,
And truly, though the truth is like a jest,
I could not choose but fancy, half the way,　　400
I stood alone i' the belfry, fifty bells

Of naked iron, mad with merriment
(As one who laughs and cannot stop himself),
All clanking at me, in me, over me,
Until I shrieked a shriek I could not hear,
And swooned with noise, — but still, along my swoon,
Was 'ware the baffled changes backward rang,
Prepared, at each emerging sense, to beat
And crash it out with clangour.   I was weak;
I struggled for the posture of my soul   410
In upright consciousness of place and time,
But evermore, 'twixt waking and sleeping,
Slipped somehow, staggered, caught at Marian's eyes
A moment (it is very good for strength
To know that some one needs you to be strong),
And so recovered what I called myself,
For that time.
              I just knew it when we swept
Above the old roofs of Dijon : Lyons dropped
A spark into the night, half trodden out
Unseen.   But presently the winding Rhône   420
Washed out the moonlight large along his banks
Which strained their yielding curves out clear and
       clean
To hold it, — shadow of town and castle blurred
Upon the hurrying river.   Such an air
Blew thence upon the forehead — half an air
And half a water — that I leaned and looked,
Then, turning back on Marian, smiled to mark
That she looked only on her child, who slept,
His face toward the moon too.
                          So we passed
The liberal open country and the close,   430
And shot through tunnels, like a lightning-wedge
By great Thor-hammers driven through the rock,

Which, quivering through the intestine blackness,
      splits,
And lets it in at once : the train swept in
Athrob with effort, trembling with resolve,
The fierce denouncing whistle wailing on
And dying off smothered in the shuddering dark,
While we, self-awed, drew troubled breath, oppressed
As other Titans underneath the pile
And nightmare of the mountains.   Out, at last,   440
To catch the dawn afloat upon the land !
— Hills, slung forth broadly and gauntly everywhere,
Not cramped in their foundations, pushing wide
Rich outspreads of the vineyards and the corn
(As if they entertained i' the name of France),
While down their straining sides streamed manifest
A soil as red as Charlemagne's knightly blood,
To consecrate the verdure.   Some one said
" Marseilles ! " And lo, the city of Marseilles,
With all her ships behind her, and beyond,   450
The scimitar of ever-shining sea
For right-hand use, bared blue against the sky !

That night we spent between the purple heaven
And purple water : I think Marian slept ;
But I, as a dog a-watch for his master's foot,
Who cannot sleep or eat before he hears,
I sat upon the deck and watched the night
And listened through the stars for Italy.
Those marriage-bells I spoke of sounded far,
As some child's go-cart in the street beneath   460
To a dying man who will not pass the day,
And knows it, holding by a hand he loves.
I too sat quiet, satisfied with death,
Sat silent : I could hear my own soul speak,

And had my friend, — for Nature comes sometimes
And says, "I am ambassador for God."
I felt the wind soft from the land of souls ;
The old miraculous mountains heaved in sight,
One straining past another along the shore,
The way of grand dull Odyssean ghosts,   470
Athirst to drink the cool blue wine of seas
And stare on voyagers.   Peak pushing peak
They stood : I watched, beyond that Tyrian belt
Of intense sea betwixt them and the ship,
Down all their sides the misty olive-woods
Dissolving in the weak, congenial moon
And still disclosing some brown convent tower
That seems as if it grew from some brown rock,
Or many a little lighted village, dropped
Like a fallen star upon so high a point,   480
You wonder what can keep it in its place
From sliding headlong with the waterfalls
Which powder all the myrtle and orange groves
With spray of silver.   Thus my Italy
Was stealing on us.   Genoa broke with day,
The Doria's long pale palace striking out,
From green hills in advance of the white town,
A marble finger dominant to ships,
Seen glimmering through the uncertain grey of dawn.

And then I did not think, "My Italy,"   490
I thought "My father !"   O my father's house,
Without his presence ! — Places are too much,
Or else too little, for immortal man —
Too little, when love's May o'ergrows the ground ;
Too much, when that luxuriant robe of green
Is rustling to our ankles in dead leaves.
'Tis only good to be or here or there,

Because we had a dream on such a stone,
Or this or that, — but, once being wholly waked
And come back to the stone without the dream,　500
We trip upon't, — alas, and hurt ourselves ;
Or else it falls on us and grinds us flat,
The heaviest gravestone on this burying earth.
— But while I stood and mused, a quiet touch
Fell light upon my arm, and, turning round,
A pair of moistened eyes convicted mine.
" What, Marian ! is the babe astir so soon ? "
" He sleeps," she answered ; " I have crept up thrice,
And seen you sitting, standing, still at watch.　509
I thought it did you good till now, but now " . . .
" But now," I said, " you leave the child alone."
" And you're alone," she answered, — and she looked
As if I too were something.　Sweet the help
Of one we have helped ! Thanks, Marian, for such
　　help.

I found a house at Florence on the hill
Of Bellosguardo.　'Tis a tower which keeps
A post of double observation o'er
That valley of Arno (holding as a hand
The outspread city) straight toward Fiesole
And Mount Morello and the setting sun,　　520
The Vallombrosan mountains opposite,
Which sunrise fills as full as crystal cups
Turned red to the brim because their wine is red.
No sun could die nor yet be born unseen
By dwellers at my villa : morn and eve
Were magnified before us in the pure
Illimitable space and pause of sky,
Intense as angels' garments blanched with God,
Less blue than radiant.　From the outer wall

Of the garden, drops the mystic floating grey   530
Of olive-trees (with interruptions green
From maize and vine), until 'tis caught and torn
Upon the abrupt black line of cypresses
Which signs the way to Florence.   Beautiful
The city lies along the ample vale,
Cathedral, tower and palace, piazza and street,
The river trailing like a silver cord
Through all, and curling loosely, both before
And after, over the whole stretch of land
Sown whitely up and down its opposite slopes   540
With farms and villas.

                Many weeks had passed,
No word was granted. — Last, a letter came
From Vincent Carrington : — " My dear Miss Leigh,
You've been as silent as a poet should,
When any other man is sure to speak.
If sick, if vexed, if dumb, a silver piece
Will split a man's tongue, — straight he speaks and
    says
' Received that cheque.' But you ! . . . I send
    you funds
To Paris, and you make no sign at all.
Remember, I'm responsible and wait   550
A sign of you, Miss Leigh.

               " Meantime your book
Is eloquent as if you were not dumb ;
And common critics, ordinarily deaf
To such fine meanings, and, like deaf men, loth
To seem deaf, answering chance-wise, yes or no,
' It must be ' or ' it must not' (most pronounced
When least convinced), pronounce for once aright :
You'd think they really heard, — and so they do . . .
The burr of three or four who really hear   559

And praise your book aright : Fame's smallest trump
Is a great ear-trumpet for the deaf as posts,
No other being effective.   Fear not, friend ;
We think here you have written a good book,
And you, a woman !   It was in you — yes,
I felt 'twas in you : yet I doubted half
If that od-force of German Reichenbach,
Which still from female finger-tips burns blue,
Could strike out as our masculine white heats
To quicken a man.   Forgive me.   All my heart
Is quick with yours since, just a fortnight since,   570
I read your book and loved it.

                     " Will you love
My wife, too ?   Here's my secret I might keep
A month more from you ! but I yield it up
Because I know you'll write the sooner for't,
Most women (of your height even) counting love
Life's only serious business.   Who's my wife
That shall be in a month ? you ask, nor guess ?
Remember what a pair of topaz eyes
You once detected, turned against the wall,
That morning in my London painting-room ;   580
The face half-sketched, and slurred ; the eyes alone !
But you . . . you caught them up with yours, and
    said
' Kate   Ward's   eyes,   surely.' — Now   I   own   the
    truth :
I had thrown them there to keep them safe from Jove,
They would so naughtily find out their way
To both the heads of both my Danaës
Where just it made me mad to look at them.
Such eyes !   I could not paint or think of eyes
But those, — and so I flung them into paint
And turned them to the wall's care.   Ay, but now   590

I've let them out, my Kate's : I've painted her
(I change my style and leave mythologies),
The whole sweet face ; it looks upon my soul
Like a face on water, to beget itself.
A half-length portrait, in a hanging cloak
Like one you wore once ; 'tis a little frayed, —
I pressed too for the nude harmonious arm ;
But she, she'd have her way, and have her cloak —
She said she could be like you only so,
And would not miss the fortune.   Ah, my friend, 600
You'll write and say she shall not miss your love
Through meeting mine ? in faith, she would not
    change.
She has your books by heart more than my words,
And quotes you up against me till I'm pushed
Where, three months since, her eyes were : nay, in
    fact,
Nought satisfied her but to make me paint
Your last book folded in her dimpled hands
Instead of my brown palette as I wished,
And, grant me, the presentment had been newer ;
She'd grant me nothing : I compounded for   610
The naming of the wedding-day next month,
And gladly too.   'Tis pretty to remark
How women can love women of your sort,
And tie their hearts with love-knots to your feet,
Grow insolent about you against men,
And put us down by putting up the lip,
As if a man — there *are* such, let us own,
Who write not ill — remains a man, poor wretch,
While you —— !   Write weaker than Aurora Leigh,
And there'll be women who believe of you   620
(Besides my Kate) that if you walked on sand
You would not leave a foot-print.

                                 " Are you put
To wonder by my marriage, like poor Leigh ?
' Kate Ward ! ' he said. ' Kate Ward ! ' he said
    anew.
' I thought . . .' he said, and stopped — ' I did
    not think . . .'
And then he dropped to silence.
                                  " Ah, he's changed.
I had not seen him, you're aware, for long,
But went of course. I have not touched on this
Through all this letter — conscious of your heart,
And writing lightlier for the heavy fact,   630
As clocks are voluble with lead.
                             " How poor,
To say I'm sorry ! dear Leigh, dearest Leigh.
In those old days of Shropshire — pardon me —
When he and you fought many a field of gold
On what you should do, or you should not do,
Make bread or verses (it just came to that),
I thought you'd one day draw a silken peace
Through a golden ring. I thought so : foolishly,
The event proved ; for you went more opposite 639
To each other, month by month, and year by year,
Until this happened. God knows best, we say,
But hoarsely. When the fever took him first,
Just after I had writ to you in France,
They tell me, Lady Waldemar mixed drinks
And counted grains, like any salaried nurse,
Excepting that she wept too. Then Lord Howe,
You're right about Lord Howe, Lord Howe's a trump,
And yet, with such in his hand, a man like Leigh
May lose as *he* does. There's an end to all,
Yes, even this letter, though this second sheet 650
May find you doubtful. Write a word for Kate :

She reads my letters always, like a wife,
And if she sees her name I'll see her smile
And share the luck.   So, bless you, friend of two !
I will not ask you what your feeling is
At Florence with my pictures ; I can hear
Your heart a-flutter over the snow-hills :
And, just to pace the Pitti with you once,
I'd give a half-hour of to-morrow's walk
With Kate . . . I think so.   Vincent Carring-
    ton.''   660

The noon was hot ; the air scorched like the sun,
And was shut out.   The closed persiani threw
Their long-scored shadows on my villa-floor,
And interlined the golden atmosphere
Straight, still, — across the pictures on the wall,
The statuette on the console (of young Love
And Psyche made one marble by a kiss),
The low couch where I leaned, the table near,
The vase of lilies Marian pulled last night
(Each green leaf and each white leaf ruled in black 670
As if for writing some new text of fate),
And the open letter, rested on my knee,
But there the lines swerved, trembled, though I sat
Untroubled, plainly, reading it again,
And three times.   Well, he's married ; that is clear.
No wonder that he's married, nor much more
That Vincent's therefore '' sorry.''   Why, of course
The lady nursed him when he was not well,
Mixed drinks, — unless nepenthe was the drink
'Twas scarce worth telling.   But a man in love   680
Will see the whole sex in his mistress' hood,
The prettier for its lining of fair rose,
Although he catches back and says at last,

" I'm sorry."   Sorry.   Lady Waldemar
At prettiest, under the said hood, preserved
From such a light as I could hold to her face
To flare its ugly wrinkles out to shame,
Is scarce a wife for Romney, as friends judge,
Aurora Leigh or Vincent Carrington,
That's plain.   And if he's " conscious of my
    heart " . . .   690
It may be natural, though the phrase is strong
(One's apt to use strong phrases, being in love) ;
And even that stuff of " fields of gold," " gold
    rings,"
And what he " thought," poor Vincent, what he
    " thought,"
May never mean enough to ruffle me.
— Why, this room stifles.   Better burn than choke ;
Best have air, air, although it comes with fire,
Throw open blinds and windows to the noon,
And take a blister on my brow instead
Of this dead weight ! best, perfectly be stunned   700
By those insufferable cicale, sick
And hoarse with rapture of the summer-heat,
That sing, like poets, till their hearts break, — sing
Till men say " It's too tedious."

                          Books succeed,
And lives fail.   Do I feel it so, at last ?
Kate loves a worn-out cloak for being like mine,
While I live self-despised for being myself,
And yearn toward some one else, who yearns away
From what he is, in his turn.   Strain a step
For ever, yet gain no step ?   Are we such,   710
We cannot, with our admirations even,
Our tip-toe aspirations, touch a thing
That's higher than we ? is all a dismal flat,

And God alone above each, as the sun
O'er level lagunes, to make them shine and stink —
Laying stress upon us with immediate flame,
While we respond with our miasmal fog,
And call it mounting higher because we grow
More highly fatal ?

              Tush, Aurora Leigh !
You wear your sackcloth looped in Cæsar's way,   720
And brag your failings as mankind's.   Be still.
There *is* what's higher, in this very world,
Than you can live, or catch it.   Stand aside
And look at others — instance little Kate !
She'll make a perfect wife for Carrington.
She always has been looking round the earth
For something good and green to alight upon
And nestle into, with those soft-winged eyes,
Subsiding now beneath his manly hand
'Twixt trembling lids of inexpressive joy.   730
I will not scorn her, after all, too much,
That so much she should love me : a wise man
Can pluck a leaf, and find a lecture in't ;
And I, too, . . . God has made me, — I've a
    heart
That's capable of worship, love, and loss ;
We say the same of Shakespeare's.   I'll be meek
And learn to reverence, even this poor myself.

The book, too — pass it.   "A good book," says he,
"And you a woman."   I had laughed at that,
But long since.   I'm a woman, it is true ;   740
Alas, and woe to us, when we feel it most !
Then, least care have we for the crowns and goals
And compliments on writing our good books.
The book has some truth in it, I believe,

And truth outlives pain, as the soul does life.
I know we talk our Phædons to the end,
Through all the dismal faces that we make,
O'erwrinkled with dishonouring agony
From decomposing drugs.   I have written truth,
And I a woman, — feebly, partially,   750
Inaptly in presentation, Romney'll add,
Because a woman.   For the truth itself,
That's neither man's nor woman's, but just God's,
None else has reason to be proud of truth :
Himself will see it sifted, disenthralled,
And kept upon the height and in the light,
As far as and no farther than 'tis truth ;
For, now He has left off calling firmaments
And strata, flowers and creatures, very good,
He says it still of truth, which is His own.   760

Truth, so far, in my book ; the truth which draws
Through all things upwards — that a twofold world
Must go to a perfect cosmos.   Natural things
And spiritual, — who separates those two
In art, in morals, or the social drift,
Tears up the bond of nature and brings death,
Paints futile pictures, writes unreal verse,
Leads vulgar days, deals ignorantly with men,
Is wrong, in short, at all points.   We divide
This apple of life, and cut it through the pips :   770
The perfect round which fitted Venus' hand
Has perished as utterly as if we ate
Both halves.   Without the spiritual, observe,
The natural's impossible — no form,
No motion : without sensuous, spiritual
Is inappreciable,— no beauty or power :
And in this twofold sphere the twofold man

(For still the artist is intensely a man)
Holds firmly by the natural, to reach
The spiritual beyond it, — fixes still   780
The type with mortal vision, to pierce through,
With eyes immortal, to the antitype
Some call the ideal, — better called the real,
And certain to be called so presently
When things shall have their names. Look long
     enough
On any peasant's face here, coarse and lined,
You'll catch Antinous somewhere in that clay,
As perfect featured as he yearns at Rome
From marble pale with beauty ; then persist,
And, if your apprehension's competent,   790
You'll find some fairer angel at his back,
As much exceeding him as he the boor,
And pushing him with empyreal disdain
For ever out of sight.   Ay, Carrington
Is glad of such a creed : an artist must,
Who paints a tree, a leaf, a common stone,
With just his hand, and finds it suddenly
A-piece with and conterminous to his soul.   798
Why else do these things move him, leaf or stone ?
The bird's not moved that pecks at a spring-shoot ;
Nor yet the horse, before a quarry a-graze :
But man, the twofold creature, apprehends
The twofold manner, in and outwardly,
And nothing in the world comes single to him,
A mere itself, — cup, column, or candlestick,
All patterns of what shall be in the Mount ;
The whole temporal show related royally,
And built up to eterne significance
Through the open arms of God.   " There's nothing
     great

Nor small,'' has said a poet of our day,   810
Whose voice will ring beyond the curfew of eve
And not be thrown out by the matin's bell :
And truly, I reiterate, nothing's small !
No lily-muffled hum of a summer-bee,
But finds some coupling with the spinning stars ;
No pebble at your foot, but proves a sphere ;
No chaffinch, but implies the cherubim ;
And (glancing on my own thin, veinèd wrist)
In such a little tremor of the blood
The whole strong clamour of a vehement soul   820
Doth utter itself distinct.   Earth's crammed   with
      heaven,
And every common bush afire with God ;
But only he who sees, takes off his shoes —
The rest sit round it and pluck blackberries,
And daub their natural faces unaware
More and more from the first similitude.

Truth, so far, in my book ! a truth which draws
From all things upward.   I, Aurora, still
Have felt it hound me through the wastes of life
As Jove did Io ; and, until that Hand   830
Shall overtake me wholly and on my head
Lay down its large unfluctuating peace,
The feverish gad-fly pricks me up and down.
It must be.   Art's the witness of what Is
Behind this show.   If this world's show were all,
Then imitation would be all in art ;
There, Jove's hand gripes us ! — For we stand here,
      we,
If genuine artists, witnessing for God's
Complete, consummate, undivided work ;
That every natural flower which grows on earth   840

Implies a flower upon the spiritual side,
Substantial, archetypal, all aglow
With blossoming causes, — not so far away,
But we, whose spirit-sense is somewhat cleared,
May catch at something of the bloom and breath, —
Too vaguely apprehended, though indeed
Still apprehended, consciously or not,
And still transferred to picture, music, verse,
For thrilling audient and beholding souls
By signs and touches which are known to souls.   850
How known, they know not, — why, they cannot
     find,
So straight call out on genius, say " A man
Produced this," when much rather they should say
" 'Tis insight and he saw this."
                      Thus is Art
Self-magnified in magnifying a truth
Which, fully recognised, would change the world
And shift its morals.   If a man could feel,
Not one day, in the artist's ecstasy,
But every day, feast, fast, or working-day,
The spiritual significance burn through   860
The hieroglyphic of material shows,
Henceforward he would paint the globe with wings,
And reverence fish and fowl, the bull, the tree,
And even his very body as a man —
Which now he counts so vile, that all the towns
Make offal of their daughters for its use,
On summer-nights, when God is sad in heaven
To think what goes on in His recreant world
He made quite other ; while that moon He made
To shine there, at the first love's covenant,   870
Shines still, convictive as a marriage-ring
Before adulterous eyes.

　　　　　　　　　　How sure it is,
That, if we say a true word instantly
We feel 'tis God's, not ours, and pass it on
Like bread at sacrament we taste and pass
Nor handle for a moment, as indeed
We dared to set up any claim to such !
And I — my poem, — let my readers talk.
I'm closer to it — I can speak as well :
I'll say with Romney, that the book is weak,　　880
The range uneven, the points of sight obscure,
The music interrupted.
　　　　　　　　　Let us go.
The end of woman (or of man, I think)
Is not a book.　Alas, the best of books
Is but a word in Art, which soon grows cramped,
Stiff, dubious-statured with the weight of years,
And drops an accent or digamma down
Some cranny of unfathomable time,
Beyond the critic's reaching.　Art itself,
We've called the larger life, must feel the soul　890
Live past it.　For more's felt than is perceived,
And more's perceived than can be interpreted,
And Love strikes higher with his lambent flame
Than Art can pile the faggots.
　　　　　　　　　　Is it so ?
When Jove's hand meets us with composing touch,
And when at last we are hushed and satisfied,
Then Io does not call it truth, but love ?
Well, well ! my father was an Englishman :
My mother's blood in me is not so strong
That I should bear this stress of Tuscan noon　900
And keep my wits.　The town, there, seems to seethe
In this Medæan boil-pot of the sun,
And all the patient hills are bubbling round

As if a prick would leave them flat.   Does heaven
Keep far off, not to set us in a blaze ?
Not so, — let drag your fiery fringes, heaven,
And burn us up to quiet.   Ah, we know
Too much here, not to know what's best for peace ;
We have too much light here, not to want more fire
To purify and end us.   We talk, talk,   910
Conclude upon divine philosophies,
And get-the thanks of men for hopeful books,
Whereat we take our own life up, and . . . pshaw !
Unless we piece it with another's life
(A yard of silk to carry out our lawn)
As well suppose my little handkerchief
Would cover Samminiato, church and all,
If out I threw it past the cypresses,
As, in this ragged, narrow life of mine,
Contain my own conclusions.

                 But at least   920
We'll shut up the persiani and sit down,
And when my head's done aching, in the cool,
Write just a word to Kate and Carrington.
May joy be with them ! she has chosen well,
And he not ill.

            I should be glad, I think,
Except for Romney.   Had *he* married Kate,
I surely, surely, should be very glad.
This Florence sits upon me easily,
With native air and tongue.   My graves are calm,
And do not too much hurt me.   Marian's good, 930
Gentle and loving, — lets me hold the child,
Or drags him up the hills to find me flowers
And fill these vases ere I'm quite awake, —
My grandiose red tulips, which grow wild,
Or Dante's purple lilies, which he blew

To a larger bubble with his prophet breath,
Or one of those tall flowering reeds that stand
In Arno, like a sheaf of sceptres left
By some remote dynasty of dead gods
To suck the stream for ages and get green,   940
And blossom wheresoe'er a hand divine
Had warmed the place with ichor.   Such I find
At early morning laid across my bed,
And wake up pelted with a childish laugh
Which even Marian's low precipitous " hush "
Has vainly interposed to put away, —
While I, with shut eyes, smile and motion for
The dewy kiss that's very sure to come
From mouth and cheeks, the whole child's face at
     once
Dissolved on mine, — as if a nosegay burst   950
Its string with the weight of roses overblown,
And dropped upon me.   Surely I should be glad.
The little creature almost loves me now,
And calls my name, " Alola," stripping off
The *r*'s like thorns, to make it smooth enough
To take between his dainty, milk-fed lips,
God love him !   I should certainly be glad,
Except, God help me, that I'm sorrowful
Because of Romney.
                    Romney, Romney !   Well,
This grows absurd ! — too like a tune that runs   960
I' the head, and forces all things in the world,
Wind, rain, the creaking gnat, or stuttering fly,
To sing itself and vex you, — yet perhaps
A paltry tune you never fairly liked,
Some " I'd be a butterfly," or " C'est l'amour : "
We're made so, — not such tyrants to ourselves
But still we are slaves to nature.   Some of us

Are turned, too, overmuch like some poor verse
With a trick of ritournelle : the same thing goes
And comes back ever.

             Vincent Carrington   970
Is "sorry," and I'm sorry ; but *he*'s strong
To mount from sorrow to his heaven of love,
And when he says at moments, "Poor, poor Leigh,
Who'll never call his own so true a heart,
So fair a face even," — he must quickly lose
The pain of pity, in the blush he makes
By his very pitying eyes. The snow, for him,
Has fallen in May and finds the whole earth warm,
And melts at the first touch of the green grass.
But Romney, — he has chosen, after all.   980
I think he had as excellent a sun
To see by, as most others, and perhaps
Has scarce seen really worse than some of us
When all's said. Let him pass. I'm not too much
A woman, not to be a man for once
And bury all my Dead like Alaric,
Depositing the treasures of my soul
In this drained watercourse, then letting flow
The river of life again with commerce-ships
And pleasure-barges full of silks and songs.   990
Blow, winds, and help us.

                Ah, we mock ourselves
With talking of the winds ; perhaps as much
With other resolutions. How it weighs,
This hot, sick air ! and how I covet here
The Dead's provision on the river-couch,
With silver curtains drawn on tinkling rings !
Or else their rest in quiet crypts, — laid by
From heat and noise ; — from those cicale, say,
And this more vexing heart-beat.

So it is :
We covet for the soul, the body's part,   1000
To die and rot.   Even so, Aurora, ends
Our aspiration who bespoke our place
So far in the east.   The occidental flats
Had fed us fatter, therefore ? we have climbed
Where herbage ends ? we want the beast's part now
And tire of the angel's ? — Men define a man,
The creature who stands frontward to the stars,
The creature who looks inward to himself,   1008
The tool-wright, laughing creature.   'Tis enough :
We'll say instead, the inconsequent creature, man,
For that's his specialty.   What creature else
Conceives the circle, and then walks the square ?
Loves things proved bad, and leaves a thing proved
        good ?
You think the bee makes honey half a year,
To loathe the comb in winter and desire
The little ant's food rather ?   But a man —
Note men ! — they are but women after all,
As women are but Auroras ! — there are men
Born tender, apt to pale at a trodden worm,
Who paint for pastime, in their favourite dream, 1020
Spruce auto-vestments flowered with crocus-flames.
There are, too, who believe in hell, and lie ;
There are, too, who believe in heaven, and fear :
There are, who waste their souls in working out
Life's problem on these sands betwixt two tides,
Concluding, — "Give us the oyster's part, in death."

Alas, long-suffering and most patient God,
Thou needst be surelier God to bear with us
Than even to have made us ! thou aspire, aspire
From henceforth for me ! thou who hast thyself 1030

Endured this fleshhood, knowing how as a soaked
And sucking vesture it can drag us down
And choke us in the melancholy Deep,
Sustain me, that with thee I walk these waves,
Resisting ! — breathe me upward, thou in me
Aspiring who art the way, the truth, the life, —
That no truth henceforth seem indifferent,
No way to truth laborious, and no life,
Not even this life I live, intolerable !

The days went by.   I took up the old days,   1040
With all their Tuscan pleasures worn and spoiled,
Like some lost book we dropped in the long grass
On such a happy summer-afternoon
When last we read it with a loving friend,
And find in autumn when the friend is gone,
The grass cut short, the weather changed, too late,
And stare at, as at something wonderful
For sorrow, — thinking how two hands before
Had held up what is left to only one,
And how we smiled when such a vehement nail 1050
Impressed the tiny dint here which presents
This verse in fire for ever.   Tenderly
And mournfully I lived.   I knew the birds
And insects, — which looked fathered by the flowers
And emulous of their hues : I recognised
The moths, with that great overpoise of wings
Which make a mystery of them how at all
They can stop flying : butterflies, that bear
Upon their blue wings such red embers round,
They seem to scorch the blue air into holes   1060
Each flight they take : and fire-flies, that suspire
In short soft lapses of transported flame
Across the tingling Dark, while overhead

The constant and inviolable stars
Outburn those light-of-love : melodious owls
(If music had but one note and was sad,
'Twould sound just so), and all the silent swirl
Of bats that seem to follow in the air
Some grand circumference of a shadowy dome   1069
To which we are blind : and then the nightingales,
Which pluck our heart across a garden-wall
(When walking in the town) and carry it
So high into the bowery almond trees
We tremble and are afraid, and feel as if
The golden flood of moonlight unaware
Dissolved the pillars of the steady earth
And made it less substantial.   And I knew
The harmless opal snakes, the large-mouthed frogs
(Those noisy vaunters of their shallow streams) ;
And lizards, the green lightnings of the wall,   1080
Which, if you sit down quiet, nor sigh loud,
Will flatter you and take you for a stone,
And flash familiarly about your feet
With such prodigious eyes in such small heads ! —
I knew them (though they had somewhat dwindled
      from
My childish imagery), and kept in mind
How last I sat among them equally,
In fellowship and mateship, as a child
Feels equal still toward insect, beast, and bird,
Before the Adam in him has forgone   1090
All privilege of Eden, — making friends
And talk with such a bird or such a goat,
And buying many a two-inch-wide rush-cage
To let out the caged cricket on a tree,
Saying " Oh, my dear grillino, were you cramped ?
And are you happy with the ilex-leaves ?

And do you love me who have let you go ?
Say *yes* in singing, and I'll understand.''

But now the creatures all seemed farther off,
No longer mine, nor like me, only *there*,   1100
A gulf between us. I could yearn indeed,
Like other rich men, for a drop of dew
To cool this heat, — a drop of the early dew,
The irrecoverable child-innocence
(Before the heart took fire and withered life)
When childhood might pair equally with birds ;
But now . . . the birds were grown too proud for
    us,
Alas, the very sun forbids the dew.
And I, I had come back to an empty nest,
Which every bird's too wise for. How I heard 1110
My father's step on that deserted ground,
His voice along that silence, as he told
The names of bird and insect, tree and flower,
And all the presentations of the stars
Across Valdarno, interposing still
'' My child,'' '' my child.'' When fathers say
    '' my child,''
'Tis easier to conceive the universe,
And life's transitions down the steps of law.

I rode once to the little mountain-house
As fast as if to find my father there,   1120
But, when in sight of 't, within fifty yards,
I dropped my horse's bridle on his neck
And paused upon his flank. The house's front
Was cased with lingots of ripe Indian corn
In tessellated order and device
Of golden patterns, not a stone of wall

Uncovered, — not an inch of room to grow
A vine-leaf.   The old porch had disappeared ;
And right in the open doorway sat a girl
As plaiting straws, her black hair strained away   1130
To a scarlet kerchief caught beneath her chin
In Tuscan fashion, — her full ebon eyes,
Which looked too heavy to be lifted so,
Still dropped and lifted toward the mulberry tree
On which the lads were busy with their staves
In shout and laughter, stripping every bough
As bare as winter, of those summer leaves
My father had not changed for all the silk
In which the ugly silkworms hide themselves.
Enough.   My horse recoiled before my heart ;   1140
I turned the rein abruptly.   Back we went
As fast, to Florence.

               That was trial enough
Of graves.   I would not visit, if I could,
My father's, or my mother's any more,
To see if stone cutter or lichen beat
So early in the race, or throw my flowers,
Which could not out-smell heaven or sweeten earth.
They live too far above, that I should look
So far below to find them : let me think
That rather they are visiting my grave,   1150
Called life here (undeveloped yet to life),
And that they drop upon me, now and then,
For token or for solace, some small weed
Least odorous of the growths of paradise,
To spare such pungent scents as kill with joy.

My old Assunta, too, was dead, was dead —
O land of all men's past ! for me alone,
It would not mix its tenses.   I was past,

It seemed, like others, — only not in heaven.
And many a Tuscan eve I wandered down   1160
The cypress alley like a restless ghost
That tries its feeble ineffectual breath
Upon its own charred funeral-brands put out
Too soon, where black and stiff stood up the trees
Against the broad vermilion of the skies.
Such skies ! — all clouds abolished in a sweep
Of God's skirt, with a dazzle to ghosts and men,
As down I went, saluting on the bridge
The hem of such before't was caught away
Beyond the peaks of Lucca.   Underneath,   1170
The river, just escaping from the weight
Of that intolerable glory, ran
In acquiescent shadow murmurously ;
While, up beside it, streamed the festa-folk
With fellow-murmurs from their feet and fans,
And *issimo* and *ino* and sweet poise
Of vowels in their pleasant scandalous talk ;
Returning from the grand-duke's dairy-farm
Before the trees grew dangerous at eight   1179
(For " trust no tree by moonlight," Tuscans say),
To eat their ice at Donay's tenderly, —
Each lovely lady close to a cavalier
Who holds her dear fan while she feeds her smile
On meditative spoonfuls of vanille
And listens to his hot-breathed vows of love
Enough to thaw her cream and scorch his beard.

'Twas little matter.   I could pass them by
Indifferently, not fearing to be known.
No danger of being wrecked upon a friend,
And forced to take an iceberg for an isle !   1190
The very English, here, must wait and learn

To hang the coweb of their gossip out
To catch a fly.   I'm happy.   It's sublime,
This perfect solitude of foreign lands !
To be, as if you had not been till then,
And were then, simply that you chose to be :
To spring up, not be brought forth from the ground,
Like grasshoppers at Athens, and skip thrice
Before a woman makes a pounce on you
And plants you in her hair ! — possess, yourself, 1200
A new world all alive with creatures new,
New sun, new moon, new flowers, new people — ah,
And be possessed by none of them ! no right
In one, to call your name, inquire your where,
Or what you think of Mister Someone's book,
Or Mister Other's marriage or decease,
Or how's the headache which you had last week,
Or why you look so pale still, since it's gone ?
— Such most surprising riddance of one's life
Comes next one's death ; 'tis disembodiment   1210
Without the pang.   I marvel, people choose
To stand stock-still like fakirs, till the moss
Grows on them and they cry out, self-admired,
"How verdant and how virtuous !"   Well, I'm
      glad ;
Or should be, if grown foreign to myself
As surely as to others.
                    Musing so,
I walked the narrow unrecognising streets,
Where many a palace-front peers gloomily
Through stony vizors iron-barred (prepared
Alike, should foe or lover pass that way,   1220
For guest or victim), and came wandering out
Upon the churches with mild open doors
And plaintive wail of vespers, where a few,

Those chiefly women, sprinkled round in blots
Upon the dusky pavement, knelt and prayed
Toward the altar's silver glory.   Oft a ray
(I liked to sit and watch) would tremble out,
Just touch some face more lifted, more in need
(Of course a woman's), — while I dreamed a tale
To fit its fortunes.   There was one who looked 1230
As if the earth had suddenly grown too large
For such a little humpback thing as she ;
The pitiful black kerchief round her neck
Sole proof she had had a mother.   One, again,
Looked sick for love, — seemed praying some soft
     saint
To put more virtue in the new fine scarf
She spent a fortnight's meals on, yesterday,
That cruel Gigi might return his eyes
From Giuliana.   There was one, so old,
So old, to kneel grew easier than to stand, —   1240
So solitary, she accepts at last
Our Lady for her gossip, and frets on
Against the sinful world which goes its rounds
In marrying and being married, just the same
As when 'twas almost good and had the right
(Her Gian alive, and she herself eighteen).
" And yet, now even, if Madonna willed,
She'd win a tern in Thursday's lottery
And better all things.   Did she dream for nought,
That, boiling cabbage for the fast day's soup,   1250
It smelt like blessèd entrails ? such a dream
For nought ? would sweetest Mary cheat her so,
And lose that certain candle, straight and white
As any fair grand-duchess in her teens,
Which otherwise should flare here in a week ?
Benigna sis, thou beauteous Queen of Heaven ! "

I sat there musing, and imagining
Such utterance from such faces : poor blind souls
That writhe toward heaven along the devil's trail, —
Who knows, I thought, but He may stretch His hand
And pick them up ? 'tis written in the Book   1261
He heareth the young ravens when they cry,
And yet they cry for carrion. — O my God,
And we, who make excuses for the rest,
We do it in our measure.   Then I knelt,
And dropped my head upon the pavement too,
And prayed, since I was foolish in desire
Like other creatures, craving offal-food,
That He would stop His ears to what I said,
And only listen to the run and beat   1270
Of this poor, passionate, helpless blood —

                                And then
I lay, and spoke not : but He heard in heaven.

So many Tuscan evenings passed the same.
I could not lose a sunset on the bridge,
And would not miss a vigil in the church,
And liked to mingle with the outdoor crowd
So strange and gay and ignorant of my face,
For men you know not are as good as trees.
And only once, at the Santissima,
I almost chanced upon a man I knew,   1280
Sir Blaise Delorme.   He saw me certainly,
And somewhat hurried, as he crossed himself,
The smoothness of the action, — then half bowed,
But only half, and merely to my shade,
I slipped so quick behind the porphyry plinth
And left him dubious if 'twas really I
Or peradventure Satan's usual trick
To keep a mounting saint uncanonised.

But he was safe for that time, and I too ;
The argent angels in the altar-flare   1290
Absorbed his soul next moment.   The good man !
In England we were scarce acquaintances,
That here in Florence he should keep my thought
Beyond the image on his eye, which came
And went : and yet his thought disturbed my life :
For, after that, I oftener sat at home
On evenings, watching how they fined themselves
With gradual conscience to a perfect night,
Until the moon, diminished to a curve,
Lay out there like a sickle for His hand   1300
Who cometh down at last to reap the earth.
At such times, ended seemed my trade of verse ;
I feared to jingle bells upon my robe
Before the four-faced silent cherubim
With God so near me, could I sing of God ?
I did not write, nor read, nor even think,
But sat absorbed amid the quickening glooms,
Most like some passive broken lump of salt
Dropped in by chance to a bowl of œnomel,
To spoil the drink a little and lose itself,   1310
Dissolving slowly, slowly, until lost.

EIGHTH BOOK.

ONE eve it happened, when I sat alone,
Alone, upon the terrace of my tower,
A book upon my knees to counterfeit
The reading that I never read at all,
While Marian, in the garden down below,
Knelt by the fountain I could just hear thrill
The drowsy silence of the exhausted day,

And peeled a new fig from that purple heap
In the grass beside her, turning out the red
To feed her eager child (who sucked at it   10
With vehement lips across a gap of air
As he stood opposite, face and curls a-flame
With that last sun-ray, crying " Give me, give,"
And stamping with imperious baby-feet,
We're all born princes) — something startled me,
The laugh of sad and innocent souls, that breaks
Abruptly, as if frightened at itself.
'Twas Marian laughed.   I saw her glance above
In sudden shame that I should hear her laugh,
And straightway dropped my eyes upon my book, 20
And knew, the first time, 'twas Boccaccio's tale,
The Falcon's, of the lover who for love
Destroyed the best that loved him.   Some of us
Do it still, and then we sit and laugh no more.
Laugh *you*, sweet Marian, — you've   the   right   to
        laugh,
Since God Himself is for you, and a child !
For me there's somewhat less, — and so I sigh.

The heavens were making room to hold the night,
The sevenfold heavens unfolding all their gates
To let the stars out slowly (prophesied   30
In close-approaching advent, not discerned),
While still the cue-owls from the cypresses
Of the Poggio called and counted every pulse
Of the skyey palpitation.   Gradually
The purple and transparent shadows slow
Had filled up the whole valley to the brim,
And flooded all the city, which you saw
As some drowned city in some enchanted sea,
Cut off from nature, — drawing you who gaze,

With passionate desire, to leap and plunge 40
And find a sea-king with a voice of waves,
And treacherous soft eyes, and slippery locks
You cannot kiss but you shall bring away
Their salt upon your lips. The duomo-bell
Strikes ten, as if it struck ten fathoms down,
So deep; and twenty churches answer it
The same, with twenty various instances.
Some gaslights tremble along squares and streets;
The Pitti's palace-front is drawn in fire;
And, past the quays, Maria Novella Place, 50
In which the mystic obelisks stand up
Triangular, pyramidal, each based
Upon its four-square brazen tortoises,
To guard that fair church, Buonarroti's Bride,
That stares out from her large blind dial-eyes,
(Her quadrant and armillary dials, black
With rhythms of many suns and moons) in vain
Inquiry for so rich a soul as his.
Methinks I have plunged, I see it all so clear . . .
And, O my heart, . . . the sea-king!
                                        In my ears 60
The sound of waters. There he stood, my king!

I felt him, rather than beheld him. Up
I rose, as if he were my king indeed,
And then sat down, in trouble at myself,
And struggling for my woman's empery.
'Tis pitiful; but women are so made:
We'll die for you perhaps, — 'tis probable;
But we'll not spare you an inch of our full height:
We'll have our whole just stature, — five feet four,
Though laid out in our coffins: pitiful. 70
— "You, Romney! —— Lady Waldemar is here?"

He answered in a voice which was not his.
" I have her letter ; you shall read it soon.
But first, I must be heard a little, I,
Who have waited long and travelled far for that,
Although you thought to have shut a tedious book
And farewell.   Ah, you dog-eared such a page,
And here you find me."

       Did he touch my hand,
Or but my sleeve ? I trembled, hand and foot, — 79
He must have touched me. — " Will you sit ? " I asked,
And motioned to a chair ; but down he sat,
A little slowly, as a man in doubt,
Upon the couch beside me, — couch and chair
Being wheeled upon the terrace.

        " You are come,
My cousin Romney ? — this is wonderful.
But all is wonder on such summer-nights ;
And nothing should surprise us any more,
Who see that miracle of stars.   Behold."

I signed above, where all the stars were out,
As if an urgent heat had started there   90
A secret writing from a sombre page,
A blank, last moment, crowded suddenly
With hurrying splendours.

      " Then you do not know " —
He murmured.

     " Yes, I know," I said, " I know.
I had the news from Vincent Carrington.
And yet I did not think you'd leave the work
In England, for so much even, — though of course
You'll make a work-day of your holiday,
And turn it to our Tuscan people's use, —
Who much need helping since the Austrian boar   100

(So bold to cross the Alp to Lombardy
And dash his brute front unabashed against
The steep snow-bosses of that shield of God
Who soon shall rise in wrath and shake it clear)
Came hither also, raking up our grape
And olive gardens with his tyrannous tusk,
And rolling on our maize with all his swine.''

'' You had the news from Vincent Carrington,''
He echoed, — picking up the phrase beyond,
As if he knew the rest was merely talk   110
To fill a gap and keep out a strong wind ;
'' You had, then, Vincent's personal news ? ''
                                        '' His own,''
I answered.   '' All that ruined world of yours
Seems crumbling into marriage.   Carrington
Has chosen wisely.''
                    '' Do you take it so ? ''
He cried, '' and is it possible at last ''   . . .
He paused there, — and then, inward to himself,
'' Too much at last, too late ! — yet certainly ''   . . .
(And there his voice swayed as an Alpine plank
That feels a passionate torrent underneath)   120
'' The knowledge, had I known it first or last,
Could scarce have changed the actual case for *me*.
And best for *her* at this time.''
                              Nay, I thought,
He loves Kate Ward, it seems, now, like a man,
Because he has married Lady Waldemar !
Ah, Vincent's letter said how Leigh was moved
To hear that Vincent was betrothed to Kate.
With what cracked pitchers go we to deep wells
In this world !   Then I spoke, — '' I did not think,
My cousin, you had ever known Kate Ward.''   130

" In fact, I never knew her.   'Tis enough
That Vincent did, and therefore chose his wife
For other reasons than those topaz eyes
We've heard of.   Not to undervalue them,
For all that.   One takes up the world with eyes."

— Including Romney Leigh, I thought again,
Albeit he knows them only by repute.
How vile must all men be, since *he*'s a man.

His deep pathetic voice, as if he guessed
I did not surely love him, took the word ;   140
" You never got a letter from Lord Howe
A month back, dear Aurora ? "

        " None," I said.

" I felt it was so," he replied : " yet, strange !
Sir Blaise Delorme has passed through Florence ? "

           " Ay,

By chance I saw him in Our Lady's church
(I saw him, mark you, but he saw not me),
Clean-washed in holy water from the count
Of things terrestrial, — letters, and the rest ;
He had crossed us out together with his sins.   149
Ay, strange ; but only strange that good Lord Howe
Preferred him to the post because of pauls.
For me I'm sworn to never trust a man —
At least with letters."

      " There were facts to tell,
To smooth with eye and accent.   Howe sup-
  posed . . .
Well, well, no matter ! there was dubious need ;
You heard the news from Vincent Carrington.
And yet perhaps you had been startled less

To see me, dear Aurora, if you had read
That letter."
       — Now he sets me down as vexed.
I think I've draped myself in woman's pride   160
To a perfect purpose.   Oh, I'm vexed, it seems !
My friend Lord Howe deputes his friend Sir Blaise
To break as softly as a sparrow's egg
That lets a bird out tenderly, the news
Of Romney's marriage to a certain saint ;
To *smooth with eye and accent,* — indicate
His possible presence.   Excellently well
You've played your part, my Lady Waldemar, —
As I've played mine.
       "Dear Romney," I began,
"You did not use, of old, to be so like   170
A Greek king coming from a taken Troy,
'Twas needful that precursors spread your path
With three-piled carpets, to receive your foot
And dull the sound of't.   For myself, be sure,
Although it frankly grinds the gravel here,
I still can bear it.   Yet I'm sorry too
To lose this famous letter, which Sir Blaise
Has twisted to a lighter absently
To fire some holy taper : dear Lord Howe
Writes letters good for all things but to lose ;   180
And many a flower of London gossipry
Has dropped wherever such a stem broke off.
Of course I feel that, lonely among my vines,
Where nothing's talked of, save the blight again,
And no more Chianti !   Still the letter's use
As preparation . . . . . Did I start indeed ?
Last night I started at a cockchafer,
And shook a half-hour after.   Have you learnt
No more of women, 'spite of privilege,

Than still to take account too seriously   190
Of such weak flutterings ?   Why, we like it, sir,
We get our powers and our effects that way :
The trees stand stiff and still at time of frost,
If no wind tears them ; but, let summer come,
When trees are happy, — and a breath avails
To set them trembling through a million leaves
In luxury of emotion.   Something less
It takes to move a woman : let her start
And shake at pleasure, — nor conclude at yours,
The winter's bitter, — but the summer's green.''   200

He answered :   '' Be the summer ever green
With you, Aurora ! — though you sweep your sex
With somewhat bitter gusts from where you live
Above them, — whirling downward from your heights
Your very own pine-cones, in a grand disdain
Of the lowland burrs with which you scatter them.
So high and cold to others and yourself,
A little less to Romney were unjust,
And thus, I would not have you.   Let it pass :
I feel content so.   You can bear indeed   210
My sudden step beside you : but for me,
'Twould move me sore to hear your softened voice, —
Aurora's voice, — if softened unaware
In pity of what I am.''
                              Ah friend, I thought,
As husband of the Lady Waldemar
You're granted very sorely pitiable !
And yet Aurora Leigh must guard her voice
From softening in the pity of your case,
As if from lie or license.   Certainly
We'll soak up all the slush and soil of life   220
With softened voices, ere we come to *you*.

At which I interrupted my own thought
And spoke out calmly.   " Let us ponder, friend,
Whate'er our state we must have made it first ;
And though the thing displease us, ay, perhaps
Displease us warrantably, never doubt
That other states, thought possible once, and then
Rejected by the instinct of our lives,
If then adopted had displeased us more
Than this in which the choice, the will, the love, 230
Has stamped the honour of a patent act
From henceforth.   What we choose may not be good,
But, that we choose it, proves it good for *us*
Potentially, fantastically, now
Or last year, rather than a thing we saw,
And saw no need for choosing.   Moths will burn
Their wings, — which proves that light is good for
      moths,
Who else had flown not where they agonise."

" Ay, light is good," he echoed, and there paused ;
And then abruptly, . . . " Marian.   Marian's
      well ? "   240

I bowed my head but found no word.   'Twas hard
To speak of *her* to Lady Waldemar's
New husband.   How much did he know, at last ?
How much ? how little ? —— He would take no
      sign,
But straight repeated, — " Marian.   Is she well ? "

" She's well," I answered.
                                        She was there in sight
An hour back, but the night had drawn her home,
Where still I heard her in an upper room,

Her low voice singing to the child in bed,
Who, restless with the summer-heat and play   250
And slumber snatched at noon, was long sometimes
In falling off, and took a score of songs
And mother-hushes ere saw she him sound.

" She's well," I answered.
             " Here ? " he asked.
                     " Yes, here."

He stopped and sighed.   " That shall be presently,
But now this must be.   I have words to say,
And would be alone to say them, I with you,
And no third troubling."
              " Speak, then," I returned,
" She will not vex you."
               At which, suddenly
He turned his face upon me with its smile   260
As if to crush me.   " I have read your book,
Aurora."
       " You have read it," I replied,
" And I have writ it, — we have done with it.
And now the rest ? "
              " The rest is like the first,"
He answered, — " for the book is in my heart,
Lives in me, wakes in me, and dreams in me :
My daily bread tastes of it, — and my wine
Which has no smack of it, I pour it out,
It seems unnatural drinking."
                 Bitterly
I took the word up ; " Never waste your wine. 270
The book lived in me ere it lived in you ;
I know it closer than another does,
And how it's foolish, feeble, and afraid,

And all unworthy so much compliment.
Beseech you, keep your wine, — and, when you drink,
Still wish some happier fortune to a friend,
Than even to have written a far better book."

He answered gently, " That is consequent :
The poet looks beyond the book he has made,
Or else he had not made it.   If a man   280
Could make a man, he'd henceforth be a god
In feeling what a little thing is man :
It is not my case.   And this special book,
I did not make it, to make light of it :
It stands above my knowledge, draws me up ;
'Tis high to me.   It may be that the book
Is not so high, but I so low, instead ;
Still high to me.   I mean no compliment :
I will not say there are not, young or old,
Male writers, ay, or female, let it pass,   290
Who'll write us richer and completer books.
A man may love a woman perfectly,
And yet by no means ignorantly maintain
A thousand women have not larger eyes :
Enough that she alone has looked at him
With eyes that, large or small, have won his soul.
And so, this book, Aurora, — so, your book."

"Alas," I answered, "is it so, indeed ?"
And then was silent.
                        "Is it so, indeed,"
He echoed, " that *alas* is all your word ? "   300
I said, " I'm thinking of a far-off June,
When you and I, upon my birthday once,
Discoursed of life and art, with both untried.
I'm thinking, Romney, how 'twas morning then,

And now 'tis night.''

            '' And now,'' he said, '' 'tis night.''

'' I'm thinking,'' I resumed, '' 'tis somewhat sad,
That if I had known, that morning in the dew,
My cousin Romney would have said such words
On such a night at close of many years,
In speaking of a future book of mine,   310
It would have pleased me better as a hope,
Than as an actual grace it can at all :
That's sad, I'm thinking.''

            '' Ay,'' he said, '' 'tis night.''

'' And there,'' I added lightly, '' are the stars !
And here, we'll talk of stars and not of books.''

'' You have the stars,'' he murmured, — '' it is well :
Be like them ! shine, Aurora, on my dark,
Though high and cold and only like a star,
And for this short night only, — you, who keep
The same Aurora of the bright June-day   320
That withered up the flowers before my face,
And turned me from the garden evermore
Because I was not worthy.   Oh, deserved,
Deserved ! that I, who verily had not learnt
God's lesson half, attaining as a dunce
To obliterate good words with fractious thumbs
And cheat myself of the context, — *I* should push
Aside, with male ferocious impudence,
The world's Aurora who had conned her part
On the other side the leaf ! ignore her so,   330
Because she was a woman and a queen,
And had no beard to bristle through her song,
My teacher, who has taught me with a book,

My   Miriam,   whose   sweet   mouth,   when   nearly
    drowned
I still heard singing on the shore !   Deserved,
That here I should look up unto the stars
And miss the glory '' . . .

                    '' Can I understand ? ''
I broke in.   '' You speak wildly, Romney Leigh,
Or I hear wildly.   In that morning-time
We recollect, the roses were too red,   340
The trees too green, reproach too natural
If one should see not what the other saw :
And now, it's night, remember ; we have shades
In place of colours ; we are now grown cold,
And old, my cousin Romney.   Pardon me, —
I'm very happy that you like my book,
And very sorry that I quoted back
A ten years' birthday.   'Twas so mad a thing
In any woman, I scarce marvel much
You took it for a venturous piece of spite,   350
Provoking such excuses as indeed
I cannot call you slack in.''

                    '' Understand,''
He answered sadly, '' something, if but so.
This night is softer than an English day,
And men may well come hither when they're sick,
To draw in easier breath from larger air.
'Tis thus with me ; I come to you, — to you
My Italy of women, just to breathe
My soul out once before you, ere I go,
As humble as God makes me at the last   360
(I thank Him), quite out of the way of men
And yours, Aurora, — like a punished child,
His cheeks all blurred with tears and naughtiness,
To silence in a corner.   I am come

To speak, beloved" . . .

                "Wisely, cousin Leigh,
And worthily of us both ! "

                  "Yes, worthily ;
For this time I must speak out and confess
That I, so truculent in assumption once,
So absolute in dogma, proud in aim,
And fierce in expectation, — I, who felt   370
The whole world tugging at my skirts for help,
As if no other man than I could pull,
Nor woman but I led her by the hand,
Nor cloth hold but I had it in my coat,
Do know myself to-night for what I was
On that June-day, Aurora.   Poor bright day,
Which meant the best . . . a woman and a rose,
And which I smote upon the cheek with words
Until it turned and rent me !   Young you were,
That birthday, poet, but you talked the right :   380
While I, . . . I built up follies like a wall
To intercept the sunshine and your face.
Your face ! that's worse."

               "Speak wisely, cousin Leigh."

"Yes, wisely, dear Aurora, though too late :
But then, not wisely.   I was heavy then,
And stupid, and distracted with the cries
Of tortured prisoners in the polished brass
Of that Phalarian bull, society,
Which seems to bellow bravely like ten bulls,
But, if you listen, moans and cries instead   390
Despairingly, like victims tossed and gored
And trampled by their hoofs.   I heard the cries
Too close : I could not hear the angels lift
A fold of rustling air, nor what they said

To help my pity.   I beheld the world
As one great famishing carnivorous mouth, —
A huge, deserted, callow, blind bird Thing,
With piteous open beak that hurt my heart,
Till down upon the filthy ground I dropped,
And tore the violets up to get the worms.   400
Worms, worms, was all my cry : an open mouth,
A gross want, bread to fill it to the lips,
No more.   That poor men narrowed their demands
To such an end, was virtue, I supposed,
Adjudicating that to see it so
Was reason.   Oh, I did not push the case
Up higher, and ponder how it answers when
The rich take up the same cry for themselves,
Professing equally, — ' An open mouth,
A gross need, food to fill us, and no more.'   410
Why that's so far from virtue, only vice
Can find excuse for't that makes libertines,
And slurs our cruel streets from end to end
With eighty thousand women in one smile,
Who only smile at night beneath the gas.
The body's satisfaction and no more,
Is used for argument against the soul's
Here too ; the want, here too, implies the right.
— How dark I stood that morning in the sun,
My best Aurora (though I saw your eyes),   420
When first you told me . . . oh, I recollect
The sound, and how you lifted your small hand,
And how your white dress and your burnished curls
Went greatening round you in the still blue air,
As if an inspiration from within
Had blown them all out when you spoke the words,
Even these, — ' You will not compass your poor
       ends

'Of barley-feeding and material ease,
'Without the poet's individualism
'To work your universal.   It takes a soul   430
'To move a body, — it takes a high-souled man
'To move the masses, even to a cleaner stye :
'It takes the ideal, to blow an inch inside
'The dust of the actual : and your Fouriers failed,
'Because not poets enough to understand
'That life develops from within.'   I say
Your words, — I could say other words of yours,
For none of all your words will let me go ;
Like sweet verbena which, being brushed against,
Will hold us three hours after by the smell   440
In spite of long walks upon windy hills.
But these words dealt in sharper perfume, — these
Were ever on me, stinging through my dreams,
And saying themselves for ever o'er my acts
Like some unhappy verdict.   That I failed,
Is certain.   Stye or no stye, to contrive
The swine's propulsion toward the precipice,
Proved easy and plain.   I subtly organised
And ordered, built the cards up high and higher,
Till, some one breathing, all fell flat again ;   450
In setting right society's wide wrong,
Mere life's so fatal.   So I failed indeed
Once, twice, and oftener, — hearing through the rents
Of obstinate purpose, still those words of yours,
'*You will not compass your poor ends, not you !*'
But harder than you said them ; every time
Still farther from your voice, until they came
To overcrow me with triumphant scorn
Which vexed me to resistance.   Set down this
For condemnation, — I was guilty here ;   460
I stood upon my deed and fought my doubt,

As men will, — for I doubted, — till at last
My deed gave way beneath me suddenly
And left me what I am : — the curtain dropped,
My part quite ended, all the footlights quenched,
My own soul hissing at me through the dark,
I ready for confession, — I was wrong,
I've sorely failed, I've slipped the ends of life,
I yield, you have conquered."

                "Stay," I answered him ;
"I've something for your hearing, also.   I   470
Have failed too."

             "You ! " he said, "you're very great ;
The sadness of your greatness fits you well :
As if the plume upon a hero's casque
Should nod a shadow upon his victor face."

I took him up austerely, — " You have read
My book, but not my heart ; for recollect,
'Tis writ in Sanscrit, which you bungle at.
I've surely failed, I know, if failure means
To look back sadly on work gladly done, —
To wander on my Mountains of Delight,   480
So called (I can remember a friend's words
As well as you, sir), weary and in want
Of even a sheep-path, thinking bitterly . . .
Well, well ! no matter.   I but say so much,
To keep you, Romney Leigh, from saying more,
And let you feel I am not so high indeed,
That I can bear to have you at my foot, —
Or safe, that I can help you.   That June-day,
Too deeply sunk in craterous sunsets now
For you or me to dig it up alive, —   490
To pluck it out all bleeding with spent flame
At the roots, before those moralising stars

We have got instead, — that poor lost day, you said
Some words as truthful as the thing of mine
You cared to keep in memory ; and I hold
If I, that day, and being the girl I was,
Had shown a gentler spirit, less arrogance,
It had not hurt me.   You will scarce mistake
The point here : I but only think, you see,
More justly, that's more humbly, of myself,   500
Than when I tried a crown on and supposed . . .
Nay, laugh, sir,— I'll laugh with you ! — pray you,
          laugh,
I've had so many birthdays since that day
I've learnt to prize mirth's opportunities,
Which come too seldom.   Was it you who said
I was not changed ? the same Aurora ?   Ah,
We could laugh there, too !   Why, Ulysses' dog
Knew *him*, and wagged his tail and died : but if
I had owned a dog, I too, before my Troy,   509
And if you brought him here, . . . I warrant you
He'd look into my face, bark lustily,
And live on stoutly, as the creatures will
Whose spirits are not troubled by long loves.
A dog would never know me, I'm so changed,
Much less a friend . . . except that you're misled
By the colour of the hair, the trick of the voice,
Like that Aurora Leigh's."

                              " Sweet trick of voice !
I would be a dog for this, to know it at last,
And die upon the falls of it.   O love,
O best Aurora ! are you then so sad   520
You scarcely had been sadder as my wife ? "

" Your wife, sir ! I must certainly be changed,
If I, Aurora, can have said a thing

So light, it catches at the knightly spurs
Of a noble gentleman like Romney Leigh,
And trips him from his honourable sense
Of what befits " . . .

      " You wholly misconceive,"
He answered.

     I returned, — " I'm glad of it.
But keep from misconception, too, yourself :
I am not humbled to so low a point,   530
Not so far saddened. If I am sad at all,
Ten layers of birthdays on a woman's head
Are apt to fossilise her girlish mirth,
Though ne'er so merry : I'm perforce more wise,
And that, in truth, means sadder. For the rest,
Look here, sir : I was right upon the whole
That birthday morning. 'Tis impossible
To get at men excepting through their souls,
However open their carnivorous jaws ;
And poets get directlier at the soul   540
Than any of your œconomists — for which
You must not overlook the poet's work
When scheming for the world's necessities.
The soul's the way. Not even Christ Himself
Can save man else than as He holds man's soul ;
And therefore did He come into our flesh,
As some wise hunter creeping on his knees,
With a torch, into the blackness of a cave,
To face and quell the beast there — take the soul,
And so possess the whole man, body and soul.   550
I said, so far, right, yes : not farther, though :
We both were wrong that June-day — both as wrong
As an east wind had been. I who talked of art,
And you who grieved for all men's griefs . . .
   what then ?

We surely made too small a part for God
In these things.   What we are, imports us more
Than what we eat ; and life, you've granted me,
Develops from within.   But innermost
Of the inmost, most interior of the interne,
God claims His own, Divine humanity   560
Renewing nature, or the piercingest verse
Pressed in by subtlest poet, still must keep
As much upon the outside of a man
As the very bowl in which he dips his beard.
— And then, . . . the rest ; I cannot surely speak :
Perhaps I doubt more than you doubted then,
If I the poet's veritable charge
Have borne upon my forehead.   If I have,
It might feel somewhat liker to a crown,
The foolish green one even. — Ah, I think,   570
And chiefly when the sun shines, that I've failed.
But what then, Romney ?   Though we fail indeed,
You . . . I . . . a score of such weak workers,
      . . . He
Fails never.   If He cannot work by us,
He will work over us.   Does He want a man,
Much less a woman, think you ?   Every time
The star winks there, so many souls are born,
Who all shall work too.   Let our own be calm :
We should be ashamed to sit beneath those stars,
Impatient that we're nothing.''

                              " Could we sit 580
Just so, for ever, sweetest friend,'' he said,
" My failure would seem better than success.
And yet indeed your book has dealt with me
More gently, cousin, than you ever will !
Your book brought down entire the bright June-day,
And set me wandering in the garden-walks,

And let me watch the garland in a place
You blushed so . . . nay, forgive me, do not
    stir, —
I only thank the book for what it taught,
And what permitted.   Poet, doubt yourself,   590
But never doubt that you're a poet to me
From henceforth.   You have written poems, sweet,
Which moved me in secret, as the sap is moved
In still March branches, signless as a stone :
But this last book o'ercame me like soft rain
Which falls at midnight, when the tightened bark
Breaks out into unhesitating buds
And sudden protestations of the spring.
In all your other books, I saw but *you* :
A man may see the moon so, in a pond,   600
And not be nearer therefore to the moon,
Nor use the sight . . . except to drown himself :
And so I forced my heart back from the sight,
For what had *I*, I thought, to do with *her*,
Aurora . . . Romney ?   But, in this last book,
You showed me something separate from yourself,
Beyond you, and I bore to take it in
And let it draw me.   You have shown me truths,
O June-day friend, that help me now at night,
When June is over ! truths not yours, indeed,   610
But set within my reach by means of you,
Presented by your voice and verse the way
To take them clearest.   Verily I was wrong ;
And verily many thinkers of this age,
Ay, many Christian teachers, half in heaven,
Are wrong in just my sense who understood
Our natural world too insularly, as if
No spiritual counterpart completed it,
Consummating its meaning, rounding all

To justice and perfection, line by line,   620
Form by form, nothing single nor alone,
The great below clenched by the great above,
Shade here authenticating substance there,
The body proving spirit, as the effect
The cause : we meantime being too grossly apt
To hold the natural, as dogs a bone
(Though reason and nature beat us in the face),
So obstinately, that we'll break our teeth
Or ever we let go.   For everywhere
We're too materialistic, — eating clay   630
(Like men of the west) instead of Adam's corn
And Noah's wine — clay by handfuls, clay by lumps,
Until we're filled up to the throat with clay,
And grow the grimy colour of the ground
On which we are feeding.   Ay, materialist
The age's name is.   God Himself, with some,
Is apprehended as the bare result
Of what His hand materially has made,
Expressed in such an algebraic sign
Called God — that is, to put it otherwise,   640
They add up nature to a nought of God
And cross the quotient.   There are many even,
Whose names are written in the Christian Church
To no dishonour, diet still on mud
And splash the altars with it.   You might think
The clay Christ laid upon their eyelids when,
Still blind, He called them to the use of sight,
Remained there to retard its exercise
With clogging incrustations.   Close to heaven,
They see for mysteries, through the open doors,   650
Vague puffs of smoke from pots of earthenware,
And fain would enter, when their time shall come,
With quite another body than Saint Paul

Has promised — husk and chaff, the whole barleycorn
Or where's the resurrection ? "
                                        " Thus it is, "
I sighed.   And he resumed with mournful face,
" Beginning so, and filling up with clay
The wards of this great key, the natural world,
And fumbling vainly therefore at the lock
Of the spiritual, we feel ourselves shut in   660
With all the wild-beast roar of struggling life,
The terrors and compunctions of our souls,
As saints with lions, — we who are not saints,
And have no heavenly lordship in our stare
To awe them backward.   Ay, we are forced, so pent,
To judge the whole too partially, . . . confound
Conclusions.   Is there any common phrase
Significant, with the adverb heard alone,
The verb being absent, and the pronoun out ?
But we, distracted in the roar of life,   670
Still insolently at God's adverb snatch,
And bruit against Him that His thought is void,
His meaning hopeless, — cry, that everywhere
The government is slipping from His hand,
Unless some other Christ (say Romney Leigh)
Come up and toil and moil and change the world,
Because the First has proved inadequate,
However we talk bigly of His work
And piously of His person.   We blaspheme
At last, to finish our doxology,   680
Despairing on the earth for which He died. "

" So now, " I asked, " you have more hope of men ? "

" I hope, " he answered.   " I am come to think
That God will have His work done, as you said,

And that we need not be disturbed too much
For Romney Leigh or others having failed
With this or that quack nostrum — recipes
For keeping summits by annulling depths,
For wrestling with luxurious lounging sleeves,
And acting heroism without a scratch.   690
We fail, — what then ?   Aurora, if I smiled
To see you, in your lovely morning-pride,
Try on the poet's wreath which suits the noon
(Sweet cousin, walls must get the weather stain
Before they grow the ivy !), certainly
I stood myself there worthier of contempt,
Self-rated, in disastrous arrogance,
As competent to sorrow for mankind,
And even their odds.   A man may well despair
Who counts himself so needful to success.   700
I failed : I throw the remedy back on God,
And sit down here beside you, in good hope."

" And yet take heed," I answered, " lest we lean
Too dangerously on the other side,
And so fail twice.   Be sure no earnest work
Of any honest creature, howbeit weak,
Imperfect, ill-adapted, fails so much,
It is not gathered as a grain of sand
To enlarge the sum of human action used
For carrying out God's end.   No creature works 710
So ill, observe, that therefore he's cashiered.
The honest, earnest man must stand and work,
The woman also — otherwise she drops
At once below the dignity of man,
Accepting serfdom.   Free men freely work.
Whoever fears God, fears to sit at ease."

He cried : "True.   After Adam, work was curse :
The natural creature labours, sweats, and frets.
But, after Christ, work turns to privilege,
And henceforth, one with our humanity,   720
The Six-day Worker working still in us
Has called us freely to work on with Him
In high companionship.   So, happiest !
I count that heaven itself is only work
To a surer issue.   Let us work, indeed,
But no more work as Adam, — nor as Leigh
Erewhile, as if the only man on earth,
Responsible for all the thistles blown
And tigers couchant, struggling in amaze
Against disease and winter, snarling on   730
For ever that the world's not paradise.
O cousin, let us be content, in work,
To do the thing we can, and not presume
To fret because it's little.   'Twill employ
Seven men, they say, to make a perfect pin :
Who makes the head, content to miss the point ;
Who makes the point, agreed to leave the join ·
And if a man should cry 'I want a pin,
'And I must make it straightway, head and point,'
His wisdom is not worth the pin he wants.   740
Seven men to a pin, — and not a man too much !
Seven generations, haply, to this world,
To right it visibly a finger's breadth,
And mend its rents a little.   Oh, to storm
And say ' This world here is intolerable ;
' I will not eat this corn, nor drink this wine,
' Nor love this woman, flinging her my soul
' Without a bond for't as a lover should,
' Nor use the generous leave of happiness
' As not too good for using generously ' —   750

(Since virtue kindles at the touch of joy
Like a man's cheek laid on a woman's hand,
And God, Who knows it, looks for quick returns
From joys) — to stand and claim to have a life
Beyond the bounds of the individual man,
And raze all personal cloisters of the soul
To build up public stores and magazines,
As if God's creatures otherwise were lost,
The builder surely saved by any means !
To think, — I have a pattern on my nail, 760
And I will carve the world new after it
And solve so these hard social questions — nay,
Impossible social questions, since their roots
Strike deep in Evil's own existence here,
Which God permits because the question's hard
To abolish evil nor attaint free-will.
Ay, hard to God, but not to Romney Leigh !
For Romney has a pattern on his nail
(Whatever might be lacking on the Mount),
And, not being over-nice to separate 770
What's element from what's convention, hastes
By line on line to draw you out a world,
Without your help indeed, unless you take
His yoke upon you, and will learn of him,
So much he has to teach ! so good a world !
The same the whole creation's groaning for !
No rich nor poor, no gain nor loss nor stint ;
No pottage in it able to exclude
A brother's birthright, and no right of birth
The pottage — both secured to every man, 780
And perfect virtue dealt out like the rest
Gratuitously, with the soap at six,
To whoso does not seek it."
        "Softly, sir,"

I interrupted, — "I had a cousin once
I held in reverence.   If he strained too wide,
It was not to take honour, but give help ;
The gesture was heroic.   If his hand
Accomplished nothing . . . (well, it is not proved)
That empty hand thrown impotently out
Were sooner caught, I think, by One in heaven, 790
Than many a hand that reaped a harvest in,
And keeps the scythe's glow on it.   Pray you, then,
For my sake merely, use less bitterness
In speaking of my cousin."

                  "Ah," he said,
"Aurora ! when the prophet beats the ass,
The angel intercedes."   He shook his head —
"And yet to mean so well and fail so foul,
Expresses ne'er another beast than man ;
The antithesis is human.   Hearken, dear ;
There's too much abstract willing, purposing,   800
In this poor world.   We talk by aggregates,
And think by systems, and, being used to face
Our evils in statistics, are inclined
To cap them with unreal remedies
Drawn out in haste on the other side the slate."

"That's true," I answered, fain to throw up thought
And make a game of't.   "Yes, we generalise
Enough to please you.   If we pray at all,
We pray no longer for our daily bread,
But next centenary's harvests.   If we give,   810
Our cup of water is not tendered till
We lay down pipes and found a Company
With Branches.   Ass or angel, 'tis the same :
A woman cannot do the thing she ought,
Which means whatever perfect thing she can,

In life, in art, in science, but she fears
To let the perfect action take her part,
And rest there : she must prove what she can do
Before she does it, prate of woman's rights,
Of woman's mission, woman's function, till   820
The men (who are prating too on their side) cry,
'A woman's function plainly is . . . to talk.'
Poor souls, they are very reasonably vexed ;
They cannot hear each other talk.''

                              '' And you,
An artist, judge so ? ''

                    '' I, an artist — yes :
Because, precisely, I'm an artist, sir,
And woman, if another sat in sight,
I'd whisper, — Soft, my sister ! not a word !
By speaking we prove only we can speak,
Which he, the man here, never doubted.   What 830
He doubts is, whether we can *do* the thing
With decent grace we've not yet done at all.
Now, do it ; bring your statue, — you have room !
He'll see it even by the starlight here ;
And if 'tis e'er so little like a god
Who looks out from the marble silently
Along the track of his own shining dart
Through the dusk of ages, there's no need to speak ;
The universe shall henceforth speak for you,
And witness, 'She who did this thing was born   840
To do it — claims her license in her work.'
And so with more works.   Whoso cures the plague,
Though twice a woman, shall be called a leech :
Who rights a land's finances is excused
For touching coppers, though her hands be white.
But we, we talk ! ''

                    '' It is the age's mood,''

He said ; " we boast, and do not.   We put up
Hostelry signs where'er we lodge a day, —
Some red colossal cow with mighty paps
A Cyclops' fingers could not strain to milk, —   850
Then bring out presently our saucerful
Of curds.   We want more quiet in our works,
More knowledge of the bounds in which we work ;
More knowledge that each individual man
Remains an Adam to the general race,
Constrained to see, like Adam, that he keep
His personal state's condition honestly,
Or vain all thoughts of his to help the world,
Which still must be developed from its *one*
If bettered in its many.   We indeed,   860
Who think to lay it out new like a park,
We take a work on us which is not man's,
For God alone sits far enough above
To speculate so largely.   None of us
(Not Romney Leigh) is mad enough to say,
We'll have a grove of oaks upon that slope
And sink the need of acorns.   Government,
If veritable and lawful, is not given
By imposition of the foreign hand,
Nor chosen from a pretty pattern-book   870
Of some domestic idealogue who sits
And coldly chooses empire, where as well
He might republic.   Genuine government
Is but the expression of a nation, good
Or less good — even as all society,
Howe'er unequal, monstrous, crazed and cursed,
Is but the expression of men's single lives,
The loud sum of the silent units.   What,
We'd change the aggregate and yet retain
Each separate figure ? whom do we cheat by that ?880

Now, not even Romney.''

                                      ''Cousin, you are sad.
Did all your social labour at Leigh Hall,
And elsewhere, come to nought, then ?''

                                       ''It *was* nought,''
He answered mildly.   ''There is room, indeed,
For statues still in this large world of God's,
But not for vacuums ; so I am not sad —
Not sadder than is good for what I am.
My vain phalanstery dissolved itself ;
My men and women of disordered lives
I brought in orderly to dine and sleep,   890
Broke up those waxen masks I made them wear,
With fierce contortions of the natural face,
And cursed me for my tyrannous constraint
In forcing crooked creatures to live straight ;
And set the country hounds upon my back
To bite and tear me for my wicked deed
Of trying to do good without the church
Or even the squires, Aurora.   Do you mind
Your ancient neighbours ?   The great book-club teems
With 'sketches,' 'summaries,' and 'last tracts ' but
    twelve,   900
On socialistic troublers of close bonds
Betwixt the generous rich and grateful poor.
The vicar preached from ' Revelations ' (till
The doctor woke), and found me with ' the frogs '
On three successive Sundays ; ay, and stopped
To weep a little (for he's getting old)
That such perdition should o'ertake a man
Of such fair acres — in the parish, too !
He printed his discourses 'by request,'
And if your book shall sell as his did, then   910
Your verses are less good than I suppose.

The women of the neighbourhood subscribed,
And sent me a copy, bound in scarlet silk,
Tooled edges, blazoned with the arms of Leigh :
I own that touched me."

                " What, the pretty ones ?
Poor Romney ! ''

             " Otherwise the effect was small :
I had my windows broken once or twice
By liberal peasants naturally incensed
At such a vexer of Arcadian peace,
Who would not let men call their wives their
    own   920
To kick like Britons, and made obstacles
When things went smoothly as a baby drugged,
Toward freedom and starvation — bringing down
The wicked London tavern-thieves and drabs
To affront the blessed hillside drabs and thieves
With mended morals, quotha — fine new lives ! —
My windows paid for't.　I was shot at, once,
By an active poacher who had hit a hare
From the other barrel (tired of springeing game
So long upon my acres, undisturbed,   930
And restless for the country's virtue — yet
He missed me) ; ay, and pelted very oft
In riding through the village.　' There he goes
' Who'd drive away our Christian gentlefolk,
' To catch us undefended in the trap
' He baits with poisonous cheese, and lock us up
' In that pernicious prison of Leigh Hall
' With all his murderers !　Give another name
' And say Leigh Hell, and burn it up with fire.'
And so they did, at last, Aurora."

                       " Did ? ''   940

" You never heard it, cousin ?   Vincent's news
Came stinted, then.''

        " They did ? they burnt Leigh Hall ? ''

" You're sorry, dear Aurora ?   Yes, indeed,
They did it perfectly : a thorough work,
And not a failure, this time.   Let us grant
'Tis somewhat easier, though, to burn a house
Than build a system ; yet that's easy too
In a dream.   Books, pictures — ay, the pictures !
    What,
You think your dear Vandykes would give them pause ?
Our   proud   ancestral   Leighs,   with   those   peaked
    beards,   950
Or bosoms white as foam thrown up on rocks
From the old-spent wave.   Such calm defiant looks
They flared up with ! now nevermore to twit
The bones in the family vault with ugly death.
Not one was rescued, save the Lady Maud,
Who threw you down, that morning you were born,
The undeniable lineal mouth and chin
To wear for ever for her gracious sake,
For which good deed I saved her ; the rest went :
And you, you're sorry, cousin.   Well, for me,   960
With all my phalansterians safely out
(Poor hearts, they helped the burners, it was said,
And certainly a few clapped hands and yelled),
The ruin did not hurt me as it might —
As when for instance I was hurt one day
A certain letter being destroyed.   In fact,
To see the great house flare so . . . oaken floors
Our fathers made so fine with rushes once
Before our mothers furbished them with trains,   969
Carved wainscots, panelled walls, the favourite slide

For draining off a martyr (or a rogue),
The echoing galleries, half a half-mile long,
And all the various stairs that took you up
And took you down, and took you round about
Upon their slippery darkness, recollect,
All helping to keep up one blazing jest !
The flames through all the casements pushing forth,
Like red-hot devils crinkled into snakes,
All signifying ' Look you, Romney Leigh,
' We save the people from your saving, here,   980
' Yet so as by fire ! we make a pretty show
' Besides — and that's the best you've ever done.'
— To see this, almost moved myself to clap !
The ' vale et plaude ' came too with effect
When in the roof fell, and the fire that paused,
Stunned momently beneath the stroke of slates
And tumbling rafters, rose at once and roared,
And wrapping the whole house (which disappeared
In a mounting whirlwind of dilated flame),
Blew upward, straight, its drift of fiery chaff   990
In the face of Heaven, which blenched, and ran up
        higher."

" Poor Romney ! "

                " Sometimes when I dream," he said,
" I hear the silence after, 'twas so still.
For all those wild beasts, yelling, cursing round,
Were suddenly silent, while you counted five,
So silent, that you heard a young bird fall
From the top nest in the neighbouring rookery,
Through edging over-rashly toward the light.
The old rooks had already fled too far   999
To hear the screech they fled with, though you saw
Some flying, till, like scatterings of dead leaves

In autumn-gusts, seen dark against the sky, —
All flying, — ousted, like the House of Leigh."

" Dear Romney ! "
                        " Evidently 'twould have been
A fine sight for a poet, sweet, like you,
To make the verse blaze after.   I myself,
Even I, felt something in the grand old trees,
Which stood that moment like brute Druid gods
Amazed upon the rim of ruin, where,
As into a blackened socket, the great fire   1010
Had dropped, still throwing up splinters now and then
To show them grey with all their centuries,
Left there to witness that on such a day
The House went out."
                        " Ah ! "
                        " While you counted five,
I seemed to feel a little like a Leigh, —
But then it passed, Aurora.   A child cried,
And I had enough to think of what to do
With all those houseless wretches in the dark,
And ponder where they'd dance the next time, they
Who had burnt the viol."
                        " Did you think of that ? 1020
Who burns his viol will not dance, I know,
To cymbals, Romney."
                        " O my sweet, sad voice ! "
He cried, — " O voice that speaks and overcomes !
The sun is silent, but Aurora speaks."

" Alas," I said, " I speak I know not what :
I'm back in childhood, thinking as a child,
A foolish fancy — will it make you smile ?

I shall not from the window of my room
Catch sight of those old chimneys any more."

" No more," he answered. " If you pushed one
    day   1030
Through all the green hills to our fathers' house,
You'd come upon a great charred circle, where
The patient earth was singed an acre round ;
With one stone stair, symbolic of my life,
Ascending, winding, leading up to nought !
'Tis worth a poet's seeing. Will you go ? "

I made no answer. Had I any right
To weep with this man, that I dared to speak ?
A woman stood between his soul and mine,
And waved us off from touching evermore,   1040
With those unclean white hands of hers. Enough.
We had burnt our viols, and were silent.

                                So,
The silence lengthened till it pressed. I spoke,
To breathe : " I think you were ill afterward."

" More ill," he answered, " had been scarcely ill.
I hoped this feeble fumbling at life's knot
Might end concisely, — but I failed to die,
As formerly I failed to live, — and thus
Grew willing, having tried all other ways,
To try just God's. Humility's so good,   1050
When pride's impossible. Mark us, how we make
Our virtues, cousin, from our worn-out sins,
Which smack of them from henceforth. Is it right,
For instance, to wed here while you love there ?
And yet because a man sins once, the sin
Cleaves to him, in necessity to sin,

That if he sin not *so* to damn himself,
He sins *so*, to damn others with himself:
And thus, to wed here, loving there, becomes
A duty.   Virtue buds a dubious leaf   1060
Round mortal brows; your ivy's better, dear.
— Yet she, 'tis certain, is my very wife,
The very lamb left mangled by the wolves
Through my own bad shepherding: and could I
      choose
But take her on my shoulder past this stretch
Of rough, uneasy wilderness, poor lamb,
Poor child, poor child? — Aurora, my beloved,
I will not vex you any more to-night,
But, having spoken what I came to say,   1069
The rest shall please you.   What she can, in me —
Protection, tender liking, freedom, ease —
She shall have surely, liberally, for her
And hers, Aurora.   Small amends they'll make
For hideous evils which she had not known
Except by me, and for this imminent loss,
This forfeit presence of a gracious friend,
Which also she must forfeit for my sake,
Since, . . . drop your hand in mine a moment,
      sweet,
We're parting! —— Ah, my snowdrop, what a
      touch,
As if the wind had swept it off!   You grudge   1080
Your gelid sweetness on my palm but so,
A moment?   Angry, that I could not bear
You . . . speaking, breathing, living, side by side
With some one called my wife . . . and live, myself?
Nay, be not cruel — you must understand!
Your lightest footfall on a floor of mine
Would shake the house, my lintel being uncrossed

'Gainst angels : henceforth it is night with me,
And so, henceforth, I put the shutters up :
Auroras must not come to spoil my dark.'' 1090

He smiled so feebly, with an empty hand
Stretched sideway from me — as indeed he looked
To any one but me to give him help ;
And, while the moon came suddenly out full,
The double-rose of our Italian moons,
Sufficient plainly for the heaven and earth
(The stars struck dumb and washed away in dews
Of golden glory, and the mountains steeped
In divine languor), he, the man, appeared
So pale and patient, like the marble man 1100
A sculptor puts his personal sadness in
To join his grandeur of ideal thought,
As if his mallet struck me from my height
Of passionate indignation, I who had risen
Pale, doubting paused . . . Was Romney mad
    indeed ?
Had all this wrong of heart made sick the brain ?
Then quiet, with a sort of tremulous pride,
'' Go, cousin,'' I said coldly ; '' a farewell
Was sooner spoken 'twixt a pair of friends
In those old days, than seems to suit you now. 1110
Howbeit, since then, I've writ a book or two,
I'm somewhat dull still in the manly art
Of phrase and metaphrase. Why, any man
Can carve a score of white Loves out of snow,
As Buonarroti in my Florence there,
And set them on the wall in some safe shade,
As safe, sir, as your marriage ! very good ;
Though if a woman took one from the ledge
To put it on the table by her flowers

And let it mind her of a certain friend,   1120
'Twould drop at once (so better), would not bear
Her nail-mark even, where she took it up
A little tenderly, — so best, I say :
For me, I would not touch the fragile thing
And risk to spoil it half an hour before
The sun shall shine to melt it : leave it there.
I'm plain at speech, direct in purpose : when
I speak, you'll take the meaning as it is,
And not allow for puckerings in the silk
By clever stitches.   I'm a woman, sir —   1130
I use the woman's figures naturally,
As you the male license.   So, I wish you well.
I'm simply sorry for the griefs you've had,
And not for your sake only, but mankind's.
This race is never grateful : from the first,
One fills their cup at supper with pure wine,
Which back they give at cross-time on a sponge,
In vinegar and gall.''
                         '' If gratefuller,''
He murmured, '' by so much less pitiable !
God's self would never have come down to die, 1140
Could man have thanked Him for it.''
                                   '' Happily
'Tis patent that, whatever,'' I resumed,
'' You suffered from this thanklessness of men,
You sink no more than Moses' bulrush-boat
When once relieved of Moses, — for you're light,
You're light, my cousin ! which is well for you,
And manly.   For myself, now mark me, sir,
They burnt Leigh Hall ; but if, consummated
To devils, heightened beyond Lucifers,
They had burnt, instead, a star or two of those 1150
We saw above there just a moment back,

Before the moon abolished them, — destroyed
And riddled them in ashes through a sieve
On the head of the foundering universe — what then ?
If you and I remained still you and I,
It could not shift our places as mere friends,
Nor render decent you should toss a phrase
Beyond the point of actual feeling !   Nay,
You shall not interrupt me : as you said,
We're parting.   Certainly, not once nor twice 1160
To-night you've mocked me somewhat, or yourself,
And I, at least, have not deserved it so
That I should meet it unsurprised.   But now,
Enough : we're parting . . . parting.   Cousin
     Leigh,
I wish you well through all the acts of life
And life's relations, wedlock not the least,
And it shall ' please me,' in your words, to know
You yield your wife, protection, freedom, ease,
And very tender liking.   May you live
So happy with her, Romney, that your friends 1170
Shall praise her for it !   Meantime some of us
Are wholly dull in keeping ignorant
Of what she has suffered by you, and what debt
Of sorrow your rich love sits down to pay :
But if 'tis sweet for love to pay its debt,
'Tis sweeter still for love to give its gift,
And you, be liberal in the sweeter way,
You can, I think.   At least, as touches me,
You owe her, cousin Romney, no amends :
She is not used to hold my gown so fast,   1180
You need entreat her now to let it go ;
The lady never was a friend of mine,
Nor capable, — I thought you knew as much, —
Of losing for your sake so poor a prize

As such a worthless friendship. Be content,
Good cousin, therefore, both for her and you !
I'll never spoil your dark, nor dull your noon,
Nor vex you when you're merry or at rest :
You shall not need to put a shutter up
To keep out this Aurora, — though your north   1190
Can make Auroras which vex nobody,
Scarce known from night, I fancied ! let me add,
My larks fly higher than some windows.   Well,
You've read your Leighs.   Indeed, 'twould shake a
     house,
If such as I came in with outstretched hand,
Still warm and thrilling from the clasp of one . . .
Of one we know, . . . to acknowledge, palm to palm,
As mistress there, the Lady Waldemar.''
'' Now God be with us '' . . . with a sudden clash
Of voice he interrupted.   '' What name's that ? 1200
You spoke a name, Aurora.''
                                   '' Pardon me ;
I would that, Romney, I could name your wife
Nor wound you, yet be worthy.''
                                        '' Are we mad ?''
He echoed.   '' Wife ! mine ! Lady Waldemar !
I think you said my wife.''   He sprang to his feet,
And threw his noble head back toward the moon
As one who swims against a stormy sea,
Then laughed with such a helpless, hopeless scorn,
I stood and trembled.
                         '' May God judge me so,''
He said at last, — '' I came convicted here,   1210
And humbled sorely if not enough.   I came,
Because this woman from her crystal soul
Had shown me something which a man calls light :
Because too, formerly, I sinned by her

As then and ever since I have, by God,
Through arrogance of nature, — though I loved . . .
Whom best, I need not say, since that is writ
Too plainly in the book of my misdeeds :
And thus I came here to abase myself,
And fasten, kneeling, on her regent brows   1220
A garland which I startled thence one day
Of her beautiful June-youth.   But here again
I'm baffled, — fail in my abasement as
My aggrandisement : there's no room left for me
At any woman's foot who misconceives
My nature, purpose, possible actions.   What !
Are you the Aurora who made large my dreams
To frame your greatness ? you conceive so small ?
You stand so less than woman through being more,
And lose your natural instinct (like a beast)   1230
Through intellectual culture ? since indeed
I do not think that any common she
Would dare adopt such monstrous forgeries
For the legible life signature of such
As I, with all my blots — with all my blots !
At last, then, peerless cousin, we are peers —
At last we're even.   Ay, you've left your height,
And here upon my level we take hands,
And here I reach you to forgive you, sweet,
And that's a fall, Aurora.   Long ago   1240
You seldom understood me, — but before,
I could not blame you.   Then, you only seemed
So high above, you could not see below ;
But now I breathe, — but now I pardon ! — nay,
We're parting.   Dearest, men have burnt my house,
Maligned my motives ; but not one, I swear,
Has wronged my soul as this Aurora has
Who called the Lady Waldemar my wife.''

" Not married to her ! yet you said " . . .
　　　　　　　　　　　　　　　　" Again ?
Nay, read the lines " (he held a letter out)　　1250
" She sent you through me."
　　　　　　　　　　By the moonlight there
I tore the meaning out with passionate haste
Much rather than I read it.　Thus it ran.

NINTH BOOK.

EVEN thus.　I pause to write it out at length,
The letter of the Lady Waldemar.

" I prayed your cousin Leigh to take you this :
He says he'll do it.　After years of love,
Or what is called so, when a woman frets
And fools upon one string of a man's name,
And fingers it for ever till it breaks, —
He may perhaps do for her such a thing,
And she accept it without detriment
Although she should not love him any more.　　10
And I, who do not love him, nor love you,
Nor you, Aurora, — choose you shall repent
Your most ungracious letter and confess,
Constrained by his convictions (he's convinced),
You've wronged me foully.　Are you made so ill,
You woman, to impute such ill to *me* ?
We both had mothers, — lay in their bosom once.
And after all, I thank you, Aurora Leigh,
For proving to myself that there are things
I would not do — not for my life, nor him,　　20
Though something I have somewhat overdone, —
For instance, when I went to see the gods

One morning on Olympus, with a step
That shook the thunder from a certain cloud,
Committing myself vilely.   Could I think,
The Muse I pulled my heart out from my breast
To soften, had herself a sort of heart,
And loved my mortal ?   He at least loved her, —
I heard him say so : 'twas my recompense,
When, watching at his bedside fourteen days,   30
He broke out ever like a flame at whiles
Between the heats of fever, — ' Is it thou ?
' Breathe closer, sweetest mouth ! ' and when at
        last,
The fever gone, the wasted face extinct,
As if it irked him much to know me there,
He said ' 'Twas kind, 'twas good, 'twas womanly,
(And fifty praises to excuse no love) ;
' But was the picture safe he had ventured for ? '
And then, half wandering, ' I have loved her well, 39
' Although she could not love me.' — ' Say, instead,'
I answered, ' she does love you.' — 'Twas my turn
To rave : I would have married him so changed,
Although the world had jeered me properly
For taking up with Cupid at his worst,
The silver quiver worn off on his hair.
' No, no,' he murmured ; ' no, she loves me not ;
' Aurora Leigh does better : bring her book
' And read it softly, Lady Waldemar,
' Until I thank your friendship more for that
' Than even for harder service.'   So I read   50
Your book, Aurora, for an hour that day :
I kept its pauses, marked its emphasis ;
My voice, impaled upon its hooks of rhyme,
Not once would writhe, nor quiver, nor revolt ;
I read on calmly, — calmly shut it up,

Observing, ' There's some merit in the book ;
' And yet the merit in't is thrown away,
' As chances still with women if we write
' Or write not : we want string to tie our flowers,
' So drop them as we walk, which serves to show 60
' The way we went.   Good morning, Mister Leigh ;
' You'll find another reader the next time.
' A woman who does better than to love,
' I hate ; she will do nothing very well :
' Male poets are preferable, straining less
' And teaching more.'   I triumphed o'er you both,
And left him.
     " When I saw him afterward
I had read your shameful letter, and my heart.
He came with health recovered, strong though pale,
Lord Howe and he, a courteous pair of friends,   70
To say what men dare say to women, when
Their debtors.   But I stopped them with a word,
And proved I had never trodden such a road
To carry so much dirt upon my shoe.
Then, putting into it something of disdain,
I asked, forsooth, his pardon, and my own,
For having done no better than to love,
And that not wisely, — though 'twas long ago,
And had been mended radically since.
I told him, as I tell you now, Miss Leigh,   80
And proved, I took some trouble for his sake
(Because I knew he did not love the girl)
To spoil my hands with working in the stream
Of that poor bubbling nature, — till she went,
Consigned to one I trusted, my own maid
Who once had lived full five months in my house
(Dressed hair superbly), with a lavish purse,
To carry to Australia, where she had left

A husband, said she.   If the creature lied,
The mission failed : we all do fail and lie   90
More or less — and I'm sorry — which is all
Expected from us when we fail the most
And go to church to own it.   What I meant,
Was just the best for him, and me, and her . .
Best even for Marian ! — I am sorry for't,
And very sorry.   Yet my creature said
She saw her stop to speak in Oxford Street
To one . . . no matter !   I had sooner cut
My hand off (though 'twere kissed the hour before,
And promised a duke's troth-ring for the next)   100
Than crush her silly head with so much wrong.
Poor child !   I would have mended it with gold,
Until it gleamed like Saint Sophia's dome
When all the faithful troop to morning prayer :
But he, he nipped the bud of such a thought
With that cold Leigh look which I fancied once,
And broke in, ' Henceforth she was called his wife :
' His wife required no succour : he was bound
' To Florence, to resume this broken bond ;
' Enough so.   Both were happy, he and Howe,   110
' To acquit me of the heaviest charge of all — '
— At which I shot my tongue against my fly
And struck him : ' Would he carry — he was just —
' A letter from me to Aurora Leigh,
' And ratify from his authentic mouth
' My answer to her accusation ? ' — ' Yes,
' If such a letter were prepared in time.'
— He's just, your cousin, — ay, abhorrently :
He'd wash his hands in blood, to keep them clean.
And so, cold, courteous, a mere gentleman,   120
He bowed, we parted.

     " Parted.   Face no more,

Voice no more, love no more ! — wiped wholly out
Like some ill scholar's scrawl from heart and slate, —
Ay, spit on, and so wiped out utterly
By some coarse scholar !   I have been too coarse,
Too human.   Have we business, in our rank,
With blood i' the veins ?   I will have henceforth
          none,
Not even to keep the colour at my lip.
A rose is pink and pretty without blood :
Why not a woman ?   When we've played in vain 130
The game, to adore, — we have resources still,
And can play on at leisure, being adored :
Here's Smith already swearing at my feet
That I'm the typic She.   Away with Smith ! —
Smith smacks of Leigh, — and henceforth I'll admit
No socialist within three crinolines,
To live and have his being.   But for you,
Though insolent your letter and absurd,
And though I hate you frankly, — take my Smith !
For when you have seen this famous marriage tied, 140
A most unspotted Erle to a noble Leigh
(His love astray on one he should not love),
Howbeit you may not want his love, beware,
You'll want some comfort.   So I leave you Smith,
Take Smith ! — he talks Leigh's subjects, somewhat
          worse ;
Adopts a thought of Leigh's, and dwindles it ;
Goes leagues beyond, to be no inch behind ;
Will mind you of him, as a shoe-string may
Of a man : and women, when they are made like
          you,
Grow tender to a shoe-string, footprint even,   150
Adore averted shoulders in a glass,
And memories of what, present once, was loathed.

And yet, you loathed not Romney, — though you
    played
At ' fox and goose ' about him with your soul ;
Pass over fox, you rub out fox, — ignore
A feeling, you eradicate it, — the act's
Identical.

            " I wish you joy, Miss Leigh ;
You've made a happy marriage for your friend,
And all the honour well-assorted love
Derives from you who love him, whom he loves ! 160
You need not wish *me* joy to think of it ;
I have so much.   Observe, Aurora Leigh,
Your droop of eyelid is the same as his,
And, but for you, I might have won his love,
And, to you, I have shown my naked heart ;
For which three things, I hate, hate, hate you.
    Hush !
Suppose a fourth ! — I cannot choose but think
That, with him, I were virtuouser than you
Without him : so I hate you from this gulf
And hollow of my soul, which opens out   170
To what, except for you, had been my heaven,
And is, instead, a place to curse by ! Love.''

An active kind of curse. I stood there cursed,
Confounded. I had seized and caught the sense
Of the letter, with its twenty stinging snakes,
In a moment's sweep of eyesight, and I stood
Dazed. — " Ah ! not married.''

                  " You mistake,'' he said :
" I'm married. Is not Marian Erle my wife ?
As God sees things, I have a wife and child ;
And I, as I'm a man who honours God,   180
Am here to claim them as my child and wife.''

I felt it hard to breathe, much less to speak.
Nor word of mine was needed.   Some one else
Was there for answering.   "Romney," she began,
"My great good angel, Romney."

                                 Then at first,
I knew that Marian Erle was beautiful.
She stood there, still and pallid as a saint,
Dilated, like a saint in ecstasy,
As if the floating moonshine interposed
Betwixt her foot and the earth, and raised her up 190
To float upon it.   "I had left my child,
Who sleeps," she said, "and having drawn this way,
I heard you speaking, . . . friend ! — Confirm me
    now.
You take this Marian, such as wicked men
Have made her, for your honourable wife ? "

The thrilling, solemn, proud, pathetic voice.
He stretched his arms out toward that thrilling voice,
As if to draw it on to his embrace.
— "I take her as God made her, and as men
Must fail to unmake her, for my honoured wife." 200

She never raised her eyes, nor took a step,
But stood there in her place, and spoke again.
— "You take this Marian's child, which is her
    shame
In sight of men and women, for your child,
Of whom you will not ever feel ashamed ? "
The thrilling, tender, proud, pathetic voice.
He stepped on toward it, still with outstretched arms,
As if to quench upon his breast that voice.
— "May God so father me, as I do him,
And so forsake me, as I let him feel   210

He's orphaned haply. Here I take the child
To share my cup, to slumber on my knee,
To play his loudest gambol at my foot,
To hold my finger in the public ways,
Till none shall need inquire ' Whose child is this ? '
The gesture saying so tenderly ' My own.' ''

She stood a moment silent in her place ;
Then turning toward me very slow and cold : —
' And you, — what say you ? — will you blame me
　　much,
If, careful for that outcast child of mine,　　　220
I catch this hand that's stretched to me and him,
Nor dare to leave him friendless in the world
Where men have stoned me ? Have I not the right
To take so mere an aftermath from life,
Else found so wholly bare ? Or is it wrong
To let your cousin, for a generous bent,
Put out his ungloved fingers among briars
To set a tumbling bird's nest somewhat straight ?
You will not tell him, though we're innocent,
We are not harmless, . . . and that both our
　　harms　　　　　　　　　　　　　　　　　230
Will stick to his good, smooth, noble life like burrs,
Never to drop off though he shakes the cloak ?
You've been my friend : you will not now be his ?
You've known him that he's worthy of a friend,
And you're his cousin, lady, after all,
And therefore more than free to take his part,
Explaining, since the nest is surely spoilt
And Marian what you know her — though a wife,
The world would hardly understand her case
Of being just hurt and honest ; while, for him,　240
'Twould ever twit him with his bastard child

And married harlot.　Speak, while yet there's time.
You would not stand and let a good man's dog
Turn round and rend him, because his, and reared
Of a generous breed, — and will you let his act,
Because it's generous ?　Speak.　I'm bound to you,
And I'll be bound by only you, in this."

The thrilling, solemn voice, so passionless,
Sustained, yet low, without a rise or fall,
As one who had authority to speak,　　　　　250
And not as Marian.
　　　　　　　　I looked up to feel
If God stood near me, and beheld His heaven
As blue as Aaron's priestly robe appeared
To Aaron when he took it off to die.
And then I spoke : "Accept the gift, I say,
My sister Marian, and be satisfied.
The hand that gives has still a soul behind
Which will not let it quail for having given,
Though foolish worldlings talk they know not what —
Of what they know not.　Romney's strong enough
For this : do you be strong to know he's strong : 261
He stands on Right's side ; never flinch for him,
As if he stood on the other.　You'll be bound
By me ?　I am a woman of repute ;
No fly-blow gossip ever specked my life ;
My name is clean and open as this hand,
Whose glove there's not a man dares blab about
As if he had touched it freely.　Here's my hand
To clasp your hand, my Marian, owned as pure !
As pure — as I'm a woman and a Leigh ! —　　270
And, as I'm both, I'll witness to the world
That Romney Leigh is honoured in his choice
Who chooses Marian for his honoured wife."

Her broad wild woodland eyes shot out a light,
Her smile was wonderful for rapture.   "Thanks,
My great Aurora."   Forward then she sprang,
And dropping her impassioned spaniel head
With all its brown abandonment of curls
On Romney's feet, we heard the kisses drawn
Through sobs upon the foot, upon the ground — 280
"O Romney !   O my angel !   O unchanged,
Though since we've parted I have passed the grave !
But Death itself could only better *thee*,
Not change thee ! — *Thee* I do not thank at all :
I but thank God who made thee what thou art,
So wholly godlike."
                                    When he tried in vain
To raise her to his embrace, escaping thence
As any leaping fawn from a huntsman's grasp,
She bounded off and 'lighted beyond reach,
Before him, with a staglike majesty   290
Of soft, serene defiance, — as she knew
He could not touch her, so was tolerant
He had cared to try.   She stood there with her great
Drowned eyes, and dripping cheeks, and strange,
     sweet smile
That lived through all, as if one held a light
Across a waste of waters — shook her head
To keep some thoughts down deeper in her soul, —
Then, white and tranquil like a summer-cloud
Which, having rained itself to a tardy peace,
Stands still in heaven as if it ruled the day,   300
Spoke out again, — "Although, my generous friend,
Since last we met and parted you're unchanged,
And having promised faith to Marian Erle,
Maintain it, as she were not changed at all ;
And though that's worthy, though that's full of balm

To any conscious spirit of a girl
Who once has loved you as I loved you once —
Yet still it will not make her . . . if she's dead,
And gone away where none can give or take
In marriage — able to revive, return   310
And wed you — will it, Romney ? Here's the point,
My friend, we'll see it plainer : you and I
Must never, never, never join hands so.
Nay, let me say it — for I said it first
To God, and placed it, rounded to an oath,
Far, far above the moon there, at His feet,
As surely as I wept just now at yours —
We never, never, never join hands so.
And now, be patient with me ; do not think
I'm speaking from a false humility.   320
The truth is, I am grown so proud with grief,
And He has said so often through His nights
And through His mornings, ' Weep a little still,
' Thou foolish Marian, because women must,
' But do not blush at all except for sin ' —
That I, who felt myself unworthy once
Of virtuous Romney and his high-born race,
Have come to learn, — a woman, poor or rich,
Despised or honoured, is a human soul,
And what her soul is, that she is herself,   330
Although she should be spit upon of men,
As is the pavement of the churches here,
Still good enough to pray in.   And being chaste
And honest, and inclined to do the right,
And love the truth, and live my life out green
And smooth beneath his steps, I should not fear
To make him thus a less uneasy time
Than many a happier woman.   Very proud
You see me.   Pardon, that I set a trap

To hear a confirmation in your voice,   340
Both yours and yours. It is so good to know
'Twas really God who said the same before ;
And thus it is in heaven, that first God speaks,
And then His angels. Oh, it does me good,
It wipes me clean and sweet from devil's dirt,
That Romney Leigh should think me worthy still
Of being his true and honourable wife !
Henceforth I need not say, on leaving earth,
I had no glory in it. For the rest,
The reason's ready (master, angel, friend,   350
Be patient with me) wherefore you and I
Can never, never, never join hands so.
I know you'll not be angry like a man
(For *you* are none) when I shall tell the truth,
Which is, I do not love you, Romney Leigh,
I do not love you. Ah well ! catch my hands,
Miss Leigh, and burn into my eyes with yours —
I swear I do not love him. Did I once ?
'Tis said that women have been bruised to death
And yet, if once they loved, that love of theirs   360
Could never be drained out with all their blood :
I've heard such things and pondered. Did I indeed
Love once ; or did I only worship ? Yes,
Perhaps, O friend, I set you up so high
Above all actual good or hope of good
Or fear of evil, all that could be mine,
I haply set you above love itself,
And out of reach of these poor woman's arms,
Angelic Romney. What was in my thought ?   369
To be your slave, your help, your toy, your tool.
To be your love . . . I never thought of that :
To give you love . . . still less. I gave you love ?
I think I did not give **you** anything ;

I was but only yours — upon my knees,
All yours, in soul and body, in head and heart,
A creature you had taken from the ground
Still crumbling through your fingers to your feet
To join the dust she came from.   Did I love,
Or did I worship ? judge, Aurora Leigh !
But, if indeed I loved, 'twas long ago —   380
So long ! before the sun and moon were made,
Before the hells were open, — ah, before
I heard my child cry in the desert night,
And knew he had no father.   It may be
I'm not as strong as other women are,
Who, torn and crushed, are not undone from love :
It may be I am colder than the dead,
Who, being dead, love always.   But for me,
Once killed, this ghost of Marian loves no more,
No more . . . except the child ! . . . no more
      at all.   390
I told your cousin, sir, that I was dead ;
And now, she thinks I'll get up from my grave,
And wear my chin-cloth for a wedding-veil,
And glide along the churchyard like a bride
While all the dead keep whispering through the withes,
' You would be better in your place with us,
' You pitiful corruption ! '   At the thought,
The damps break out on me like leprosy
Although I'm clean.   Ay, clean as Marian Erle !
As Marian Leigh, I know, I were not clean :   400
Nor have I so much life that I should love,
Except the child.   Ah God ! I could not bear
To see my darling on a good man's knees,
And know, by such a look, or such a sigh,
Or such a silence, that he thought sometimes,
' This child was fathered by some cursèd wretch' . . .

For, Romney, angels are less tender-wise
Than God and mothers : even *you* would think
What *we* think never.   He is ours, the child ;
And we would sooner vex a soul in heaven   410
By coupling with it the dead body's thought,
It left behind it in a last month's grave,
Than, in my child, see other than . . . my child.
We only never call him fatherless
Who has God and his mother.   O my babe,
My pretty, pretty blossom, an ill wind
Once blew upon my breast ! can any think
I'd have another — one called happier,
A fathered child, with father's love and race
That's worn as bold and open as a smile,   420
To vex my darling when he's asked his name
And has no answer ?   What ! a happier child
Than mine, my best — who laughed so loud to-night
He could not sleep for pastime ?   Nay, I swear,
By life and love, that, if I lived like some,
And loved like . . . *some,* ay, loved you, Romney
      Leigh,
As some love (eyes that have wept so much, see clear),
I've room for no more children in my arms,
My kisses are all melted on one mouth,
I would not push my darling to a stool   430
To dandle babies.   Here's a hand shall keep
For ever clean without a marriage-ring,
To tend my boy until he cease to need
One steadying finger of it, and desert
(Not miss) his mother's lap, to sit with men.
And when I miss him (not he me), I'll come
And say 'Now give me some of Romney's work,
To help your outcast orphans of the world
And comfort grief with grief.'   For you, meantime,

Most noble Romney, wed a noble wife,   440
And open on each other your great souls —
I need not farther bless you.   If I dared
But strain and touch her in her upper sphere,
And say ' Come down to Romney — pay my debt ! '
I should be joyful with the stream of joy
Sent through me.   But the moon is in my face . . .
I dare not — though I guess the name he loves ;
I'm learned with my studies of old days,
Remembering how he crushed his under-lip   449
When some one came and spoke, or did not come.
Aurora, I could touch her with my hand,
And fly because I dare not.''

                              She was gone.

He smiled so sternly that I spoke in haste.
" Forgive her — she sees clearly for herself :
Her instinct's holy.''

                         " *I* forgive ! '' he said,
" I only marvel how she sees so sure,
While others '' . . . there he paused — then hoarse,
    abrupt,
" Aurora ! you forgive us, her and me ?
For her, the thing she sees, poor, loyal child,
If once corrected by the thing I know,   460
Had been unspoken, since she loves you well,
Has leave to love you : — while for me, alas !
If once or twice I let my heart escape
This night, . . . remember, where hearts slip and
    fall,
They break beside : we're parting — parting — ah !
You do not love, that you should surely know
What that word means.   Forgive, be tolerant :
It had not been, but that I felt myself

So safe in impuissance and despair,
I could not hurt you though I tossed my arms   470
And sighed my soul out.   The most utter wretch
Will choose his postures when he comes to die,
However in the presence of a queen ;
And you'll forgive me some unseemly spasms
Which meant no more than dying.   Do you think
I had ever come here in my perfect mind
Unless I had come here in my settled mind
Bound Marian's, bound to keep the bond and give
My name, my house, my hand, the things I could,
To Marian ?   For even *I* could give as much :   480
Even I, affronting her exalted soul
By a supposition that she wanted these,
Could act the husband's coat and hat set up
To creak i' the wind and drive the world-crows off
From pecking in her garden.   Straw can fill
A hole to keep out vermin.   Now, at last,
I own heaven's angels round her life suffice
To fight the rats of our society
Without this Romney : I can see it at last ;
And here is ended my pretension which   490
The most pretended.   Over-proud of course,
Even so ! — but not so stupid . . . blind . . .
      that I,
Whom thus the great Taskmaster of the world
Has set to meditate mistaken work,
My dreary face against a dim blank wall
Throughout man's natural lifetime — could pretend
Or wish . . . O love, I have loved you !   O my
      soul,
I have lost you ! — but I swear by all yourself,
And all you might have been to me these years,
If that June morning had not failed my hope —   500

I'm not so bestial, to regret that day —
This night — this night, which still to you is fair !
Nay, not so blind, Aurora.   I attest
Those stars above us which I cannot see " . . .

" You cannot " . . .
              " That if Heaven itself should stoop,
Re-mix the lots, and give me another chance,
I'd say ' No other ! ' — I'd record my blank.
Aurora never should be wife of mine."

" Not see the stars ? "
                  " 'Tis worse still, not to see,
To find your hand, although we're parting, dear. 510
A moment let me hold it ere we part ;
And understand my last words — these, at last !
I would not have you thinking when I'm gone
That Romney dared to hanker for your love
In thought or vision, if attainable
(Which certainly for me it never was),
And wished to use it for a dog to-day
To help the blind man stumbling.   God forbid !
And now I know He held you in His palm,
And kept you open-eyed to all my faults,   520
To save you at last from such a dreary end.
Believe me, dear, that, if I had known like Him
What loss was coming on me, I had done
As well in this as He has. — Farewell, you
Who are still my light, — farewell !   How late it is :
I know that, now.   You've been too patient, sweet.
I will but blow my whistle toward the lane,
And some one comes — the same who brought me
    here.
Get in — Good-night."

           " A moment.   Heavenly Christ !
A moment.   Speak once, Romney.   'Tis not true.
I nold your hands, I look into your face —   531
You see me ? "
              " No more than the blessèd stars.
Be blessèd too, Aurora.   Nay, my sweet,
You tremble.   Tender-hearted !   Do you mind
Of yore, dear, how you used to cheat old John,
And let the mice out slyly from his traps,
Until he marvelled at the soul in mice
Which took the cheese and left the snare ?   The same
Dear soft heart always !   'Twas for this I grieved
Howe's letter never reached you.   Ah, you had
     heard   540
Of illness — not the issue, not the extent :
My life, long sick with tossings up and down,
The sudden revulsion in the blazing house,
The strain and struggle both of body and soul,
Which left fire running in my veins for blood,
Scarce lacked that thunderbolt of the falling beam
Which nicked me on the forehead as I passed
The gallery-door with a burden.   Say heaven's bolt,
Not William Erle's, not Marian's father's, — tramp
And poacher, whom I found for what he was,   550
And, eager for her sake to rescue him,
Forth swept from the open highway of the world,
Road-dust and all — till, like a woodland boar
Most naturally unwilling to be tamed,
He notched me with his tooth.   But not a word
To Marian ! and I do not think, besides,
He turned the tilting of the beam my way ;
And if he laughed, as many swear, poor wretch,
Nor he, nor I supposed the hurt so deep.
We'll hope his next laugh may be merrier,   560

In a better cause."
          " Blind, Romney ? "
                    " Ah, my friend,
You'll learn to say it in a cheerful voice ;
I, too, at first desponded.   To be blind,
Turned out of nature, mulcted as a man,
Refused the daily largesse of the sun
To humble creatures !   When the fever's heat
Dropped from me, as the flame did from my house,
And left me ruined like it, stripped of all
The hues and shapes of aspectable life,
A mere bare blind stone in the blaze of day,   570
A man, upon the outside of the earth,
As dark as ten feet under, in the grave, —
Why, that seemed hard."
                 " No hope ? "
                    " A tear ! you weep,
Divine Aurora ? tears upon my hand !
I've seen you weeping for a mouse, a bird, —
But, weep for me, Aurora ?   Yes, there's hope.
Not hope of sight, — I could be learned, dear,
And tell you in what Greek and Latin name
The visual nerve is withered to the root,
Though the outer eyes appear indifferent,   580
Unspotted in their crystals.   But there's hope.
The spirit, from behind this dethroned sense,
Sees, waits in patience till the walls break up
From which the bas-relief and fresco have dropped :
There's hope.   The man here, once so arrogant
And restless, so ambitious, for his part,
Of dealing with statistically packed
Disorders (from a pattern on his nail),
And packing such things quite another way, —
Is now contented.   From his personal loss   590

He has come to hope for others when they lose,
And wear a gladder faith in what we gain . . .
Through bitter experience, compensation sweet,
Like that tear, sweetest. I am quiet now,
As tender surely for the suffering world,
But quiet, — sitting at the wall to learn,
Content henceforth to do the thing I can :
For, though as powerless, said I, as a stone,
A stone can still give shelter to a worm,
And it is worth while being a stone for that :   600
There's hope, Aurora.''

                '' Is there hope for me ?
For me ? — and is there room beneath the stone
For such a worm ? — And if I came and said . . .
What all this weeping scarce will let me say,
And yet what women cannot say at all
But weeping bitterly . . . (the pride keeps up,
Until the heart breaks under it) . . . I love, —
I love you, Romney '' . . .

               '' Silence ! '' he exclaimed.
'' A woman's pity sometimes makes her mad.
A man's distraction must not cheat his soul   610
To take advantage of it.   Yet, 'tis hard
Farewell, Aurora.''

             '' But I love you, sir ;
And when a woman says she loves a man,
The man must hear her, though he love her not,
Which . . . hush ! . . . he has leave to answer in
     his turn ;
She will not surely blame him.   As for me,
You call it pity, — think I'm generous ?
'Twere somewhat easier, for a woman proud
As I am, and I'm very vilely proud,
To let it pass as such, and press on you   620

Love born of pity, — seeing that excellent loves
Are born so, often, nor the quicklier die, —
And this would set me higher by the head
Than now I stand.   No matter : let the truth
Stand high ; Aurora must be humble : no,
My love's not pity merely.   Obviously
I'm not a generous woman, never was,
Or else, of old, I had not looked so near
To weights and measures, grudging you the power
To give, as first I scorned your power to judge   630
For me, Aurora.   I would have no gifts,
Forsooth, but God's, — and I would use *them* too
According to my pleasure and my choice,
As He and I were equals, you below,
Excluded from that level of interchange
Admitting benefaction.   You were wrong
In much ? you said so.   I was wrong in most.
Oh, most !   You only thought to rescue men
By half-means, half-way, seeing half their wants,
While thinking nothing of your personal gain.   640
But I, who saw the human nature broad
At both sides, comprehending too the soul's,
And all the high necessities of Art,
Betrayed the thing I saw, and wronged my own life
For which I pleaded.   Passioned to exalt
The artist's instinct in me at the cost
Of putting down the woman's, I forgot
No perfect artist is developed here
From any imperfect woman.   Flower from root,
And spiritual from natural, grade by grade   650
In all our life.   A handful of the earth
To make God's image ! the despised poor earth,
The healthy, odorous earth, — I missed with it
The divine Breath that blows the nostrils out

To ineffable inflatus, — ay, the breath
Which love is.   Art is much, but Love is more.
O Art, my Art, thou'rt much, but Love is more !
Art symbolises heaven, but Love is God
And makes heaven.   I, Aurora, fell from mine.
I would not be a woman like the rest,   660
A simple woman who believes in love
And owns the right of love because she loves,
And, hearing she's beloved, is satisfied
With what contents God : I must analyse,
Confront, and question ; just as if a fly
Refused to warm itself in any sun
Till such was *in Leone :* I must fret,
Forsooth, because the month was only May,   .
Be faithless of the kind of proffered love,
And captious, lest it miss my dignity,   670
And scornful, that my lover sought a wife
To use . . . to use ! O Romney, O my love,
I am changed since then, changed wholly, — for in-
        deed
If now you'd stoop so low to take my love
And use it roughly, without stint or spare,
As men use common things with more behind
(And, in this, ever would be more behind)
To any mean and ordinary end, —
The joy would set me like a star, in heaven,
So high up, I should shine because of height   680
And not of virtue.   Yet in one respect,
Just one, beloved, I am in nowise changed :
I love you, loved you . . . loved you first and
        last,
And love you on for ever.   Now I know
I loved you always, Romney.   She who died
Knew that, and said so ; Lady Waldemar

Knows that ; . . . and Marian.   I had known
    the same,
Except that I was prouder than I knew,
And not so honest.   Ay, and, as I live,
I should have died so, crushing in my hand   690
This rose of love, the wasp inside and all,
Ignoring ever to my soul and you
Both rose and pain — except for this great loss,
This great despair — to stand before your face
And know you do not see me where I stand.
You think, perhaps, I am not changed from pride
And that I chiefly bear to say such words,
Because you cannot shame me with your eyes ?
O calm, grand eyes, extinguished in a storm,
Blown out like lights o'er melancholy seas,   700
Though shrieked for by the shipwrecked, — O my
    Dark,
My Cloud, — to go before me every day
While I go ever toward the wilderness, —
I would that you could see me bare to the soul !
If this be pity, 'tis so for myself,
And not for Romney ! *he* can stand alone ;
A man like *him* is never overcome :
No woman like me counts him pitiable
While saints applaud him.   He mistook the world ;
But I mistook my own heart, and that slip   710
Was fatal.   Romney, — will you leave me here ?
So wrong, so proud, so weak, so unconsoled,
So mere a woman ! — and I love you so,
I love you, Romney —— "

                              Could I see his face,
I wept so ?   Did I drop against his breast,
Or did his arms constrain me ? were my cheeks
Hot, overflooded, with my tears — or his ?

And which of our two large explosive hearts
So shook me ? That, I know not. There were
  words   719
That broke in utterance . . . melted, in the fire,—
Embrace, that was convulsion, . . . then a kiss
As long and silent as the ecstatic night,
And deep, deep, shuddering breaths, which meant
  beyond
Whatever could be told by word or kiss.
But what he said . . . I have written day by day,
With somewhat even writing. Did I think
That such a passionate rain would intercept
And dash this last page ? What he said, indeed,
I fain would write it down here like the rest,
To keep it in my eyes, as in my ears, 730
The heart's sweet scripture, to be read at night
When weary, or at morning when afraid,
And lean my heaviest oath on when I swear
That, when all's done, all tried, all counted here,
All great arts, and all good philosophies,
This love just puts its hand out in a dream
And straight outstretches all things.
         What he said,
I fain would write. But if an angel spoke
In thunder, should we haply know much more
Than that it thundered ? If a cloud came down 740
And wrapped us wholly, could we draw its shape,
As if on the outside and not overcome ?
And so he spake. His breath against my face
Confused his words, yet made them more intense
(As when the sudden finger of the wind
Will wipe a row of single city-lamps
To a pure white line of flame, more luminous
Because of obliteration), more intense,

The intimate presence carrying in itself
Complete communication, as with souls   750
Who, having put the body off, perceive
Through simply being.   Thus, 'twas granted me
To know he loved me to the depth and height
Of such large natures, ever competent,
With grand horizons by the sea or land,
To love's grand sunrise.   Small spheres hold small
        fires,
But he loved largely, as a man can love
Who, baffled in his love, dares live his life,
Accept the ends which God loves, for his own,
And lift a constant aspect.

                              From the day   760
I brought to England my poor searching face
(An orphan even of my father's grave),
He had loved me, watched me, watched his soul in
        mine,
Which in me grew and heightened into love.
For he, a boy still, had been told the tale
Of how a fairy bride from Italy
With smells of oleanders in her hair,
Was coming through the vines to touch his hand ;
Whereat the blood of boyhood on the palm
Made sudden heats.   And when at last I came,   770
And lived before him — lived, and rarely smiled —
He smiled and loved me for the thing I was,
As every child will love the year's first flower
(Not certainly the fairest of the year,
But, in which, the complete year seems to blow),
The poor sad snowdrop, — growing between drifts,
Mysterious medium 'twixt the plant and frost,
So faint with winter while so quick with spring,
And doubtful if to thaw itself away   779

With that snow near it.   Not that Romney Leigh
Had loved me coldly.   If I thought so once,
It was as if I had held my hand in fire
And shook for cold.   But now I understood,
For ever, that the very fire and heat
Of troubling passion in him burned him clear,
And shaped, to dubious order, word and act :
That, just because he loved me over all,
All wealth, all lands, all social privilege,
To which chance made him unexpected heir,
And, just because on all these lesser gifts,   790
Constrained by conscience and the sense of wrong,
He had stamped with steady hand God's arrow-mark
Of dedication to the human need,
He thought it should be so too, with his love.
He, passionately loving, would bring down
His love, his life, his best (because the best),
His bride of dreams, who walked so still and high
Through flowery poems as through meadow-grass,
The dust of golden lilies on her feet,
That *she* should walk beside him on the rocks   800
In all that clang and hewing out of men,
And help the work of help which was his life,
And prove he kept back nothing, — not his soul.
And when I failed him, — for I failed him, I,
And when it seemed he had missed my love, he thought
" Aurora makes room for a working-noon,"
And so, self-girded with torn strips of hope,
Took up his life as if it were for death
(Just capable of one heroic aim),
And threw it in the thickest of the world, —   810
At which men laughed as if he had drowned a dog.
No wonder, — since Aurora failed him first !
The morning and the evening made his day.

But oh, the night ! oh, bitter-sweet ! oh, sweet !
O dark, O moon and stars, O ecstasy
Of darkness !   O great mystery of love,
In which absorbed, loss, anguish, treason's self
Enlarges rapture, — as a pebble dropped
In some full wine-cup overbrims the wine !
While we two sat together, leaned that night   820
So close my very garments crept and thrilled
With strange electric life, and both my cheeks
Grew red, then pale, with touches from my hair
In which his breath was, — while the golden moon
Was hung before our faces as the badge
Of some sublime inherited despair,
Since ever to be seen by only one, —
A voice said, low and rapid as a sigh,
Yet breaking, I felt conscious, from a smile,   829
"Thank God, who made me blind, to make me see !
Shine on, Aurora, dearest light of souls,
Which rul'st for evermore both day and night !
I am happy."
                    I flung closer to his breast,
As sword that, after battle, flings to sheath ;
And, in that hurtle of united souls,
The mystic motions which in common moods
Are shut beyond our sense, broke in on us,
And, as we sat, we felt the old earth spin,
And all the starry turbulence of worlds
Swing round us in their audient circles, till,   840
If that same golden moon were overhead
Or if beneath our feet, we did not know.

And then calm, equal, smooth with weights of joy,
His voice rose, as some chief musician's song
Amid the old Jewish temple's Selah-pause,

And bade me mark how we two met at last
Upon this moon-bathed promontory of earth,
To give up much on each side, then take all.
"Beloved," it sang, "we must be here to work ;
And men who work can only work for men,   850
And, not to work in vain, must comprehend
Humanity and so work humanly,
And raise men's bodies still by raising souls,
As God did first."

    "But stand upon the earth,"
I said, " to raise them (this is human too,
There's nothing high which has not first been low ;
My humbleness, said One, has made me great !)
As God did last."

    " And work all silently
And simply," he returned, "as God does all ;
Distort our nature never for our work,   860
Nor count our right hands stronger for being hoofs.
The man most man, with tenderest human hands,
Works best for men, — as God in Nazareth."

He paused upon the word, and then resumed :
" Fewer programmes, we who have no prescience.
Fewer systems, we who are held and do not hold.
Less mapping out of masses to be saved,
By nations or by sexes.   Fourier's void,
And Comte absurd, — and Cabet puerile.
Subsist no rules of life outside of life,   870
No perfect manners without Christian souls :
The Christ Himself had been no Lawgiver
Unless He had given the life, too, with the law."

I echoed thoughtfully : " The man, most man,
Works best for men, and, if most man indeed,

He gets his manhood plainest from his soul :
While obviously this stringent soul itself
Obeys the old law of development,
The Spirit ever witnessing in ours,
And Love, the soul of soul, within the soul,   880
Evolving it sublimely.   First, God's love.''

'' And next,'' he smiled, '' the love of wedded souls,
Which still presents that mystery's counterpart.
Sweet shadow-rose, upon the water of life,
Of such a mystic substance, Sharon gave
A name to ! human, vital, fructuous rose,
Whose calyx holds the multitude of leaves,
Loves filial, loves fraternal, neighbour-loves
And civic — all fair petals, all good scents,   889
All reddened, sweetened from one central Heart !''

'' Alas,'' I cried, '' it was not long ago
You swore this very social rose smelt ill.''

'' Alas,'' he answered, '' is it a rose at all ?
The filial's thankless, the fraternal's hard,
The rest is lost.   I do but stand and think,
Across the waters of a troubled life
This Flower of Heaven so vainly overhangs,
What perfect counterpart would be in sight
If tanks were clearer.   Let us clean the tubes,
And wait for rains.   O poet, O my love,   900
Since *I* was too ambitious in my deed,
And thought to distance all men in success
(Till God came on me, marked the place, and said
' Ill-doer, henceforth keep within this line,
Attempting less than others,' — and I stand
And work among Christ's little ones, content),

Come thou, my compensation, my dear sight,
My morning-star, my morning, — rise and shine,
And touch my hills with radiance not their own.
Shine out for two, Aurora, and fulfil   910
My falling-short that must be ! work for two,
As I, though thus restrained, for two, shall love !
Gaze on, with inscient vision toward the sun,
And, from his visceral heat, pluck out the roots
Of light beyond him.   Art's a service, — mark :
A silver key is given to thy clasp,
And thou shalt stand unwearied, night and day,
And fix it in the hard, slow-turning wards,
To open, so, that intermediate door
Betwixt the different planes of sensuous form   920
And form insensuous, that inferior men
May learn to feel on still through these to those,
And bless thy ministration.   The world waits
For help.   Beloved, let us love so well,
Our work shall still be better for our love,
And still our love be sweeter for our work,
And both commended, for the sake of each,
By all true workers and true lovers born.
Now press the clarion on thy woman's lip
(Love's holy kiss shall still keep consecrate)   930
And breathe thy fine keen breath along the brass,
And blow all class-walls level as Jericho's
Past Jordan, — crying from the top of souls,
To souls, that, here assembled on earth's flats,
They get them to some purer eminence
Than any hitherto beheld for clouds !
What height we know not, — but the way we know,
And how by mounting ever we attain,
And so climb on.   It is the hour for souls,
That bodies, leavened by the will and love,   940

Be lightened to redemption.   The world's old,
But the old world waits the time to be renewed,
Toward which, new hearts in individual growth
Must quicken, and increase to multitude
In new dynasties of the race of men ;
Developed whence, shall grow spontaneously
New churches, new œconomies, new laws
Admitting freedom, new societies
Excluding falsehood : HE shall make all new.''

My Romney ! — Lifting up my hand in his,   950
As wheeled by Seeing spirits toward the east,
He turned instinctively, where, faint and far,
Along the tingling desert of the sky,
Beyond the circle of the conscious hills,
Were laid in jasper-stone as clear as glass
The first foundations of that new, near Day
Which should be builded out of heaven to God.

He stood a moment with erected brows,
In silence, as a creature might who gazed, —
Stood calm, and fed his blind, majestic eyes   960
Upon the thought of perfect noon : and when
I saw his soul saw, — "Jasper first," I said ;
"And second, sapphire ; third, chalcedony ;
The rest in order : — last, an amethyst.''

NOTES.

AURORA LEIGH.

Fifth Book. This book opens with Aurora's critical meditations upon her own work and upon the art of poetry in general. She questions whether she has been able to attune herself so perfectly with the beauty and passion of nature and humanity that her poetry will make an appeal as irresistible as nature itself, holding men whether they will or not. She concludes she must have failed since she cannot even hold and move one man, who is her cousin and her friend ; therefore it behooves her to be humble.

This reminds her that the fact that a woman always wants to do something great not for itself, but in order to please some one friend, is a sign of her weakness. She must have a mediator between herself and God. Aurora declares she will not let this vile woman's way conquer her, and will follow art for art's sake and not for any man's approbation, and if she should fail, she hopes that since she has nobly striven she will be honored with truth if not with praise, though she be a woman.

She goes on to say that her ballads had been successful, but for a poet with thoughts their pace is too rapid, and on the other hand, the sonnet, while it is fitted for the expression of a thought, does not move onwards at all.

Then, though her critics praised her descriptive poem, the public was right in not caring for it, for nature must be made alive with human meaning and spiritual significance before it can awaken any feeling in the human heart.   So her pastoral, a book of " surface pictures — pretty, cold and false," failed, and she resolves to do nothing more of that sort.   As for epics, the critics say the time for them passed with the classical era, but she will not believe it, first because she is of the opinion that Homer's age was no more heroic than any other age. Every age looks unheroic to those living in it, who see only its sordid aspects and its transitional phases, just as if Mount Athos were carved into the colossal form of a man, the peasants gathering brushwood in his ear would be unaware of the human proportions, only discernible to one five miles away.

Poets, she thinks, should have a double vision which will show them the details of the times near at hand and their large significance from a distance.   She distrusts the poet who sees no glory in his own times, and has to go back to the Middle Ages for the subjects of his poems, which can therefore never be anything but dead.   The sole work of the poet, she believes, is to represent the age in which he lives — this live, throbbing age, in which she believes there is more passion than there was in the days of Roland and his knights.   If the poet thus portrays his age the following age will recognize and appreciate his records of true life.

She next considers the question of the best form for poems, and decides that the form should be the natural outcome of the spirit.   Why should a play have five acts instead of any number which will best express the growth of the action, or confine itself to literal unities when it is the essence of passion to ignore both time and place ?

Stage conventions, it is true, demand these things of a play, but whosoever writes good poetry will look only to art, regardless of critics or popularity, and if it suits mankind it will be accepted sooner or later.   She decides she will not write plays, for the drama must make its appeal to the lowest standards of taste if it is to succeed, and if it is too good to succeed and the author should gently suggest that the fault lies as much with the audience as with him, the five hundred nobodies who criticised first will be joined by the whole public. This is just, she declares, for since the author appealed to the people why say more when they condemn than when they praise. But after all she feels that the most kingly work of the poets has been done in the drama, and honoring them so highly, she fears to keep it down to the level of the footlights. It may be, she thinks, that as the drama has outgrown the conventionalities of the Greek stage, — the simulated stature, face, and speech, — so it may outgrow not only the conventionalities of the modern stage, but the necessity for stage setting at all, and find a worthier stage in the soul itself.

She perceives what might be done, but doubts her power to do it ; again sets herself seriously to work at her art, and produces another book, which she proceeds to pull to pieces. She has put her life-blood into it, but then many a fervid man writes books as cold and flat as grave-yard stones. Art must manipulate human passion and suffering in such a way that its agony and ecstasy shall appear palpable and living. Nor would this indicate lack of feeling on the artist's part, because he has a double life, his own personal life and his perception and sympathy with the life of passion around him — "the round of crystal conscience." But in the midst of her flight describing how poets must feel she recollects that "poet" is a word soon said and a book a thing soon written, and concludes that though there is some passion in her book it takes more than passion to make either a man or book. So she feels sad, and doubts whether her work is worth while, although she gets much praise, and lovers read her lines and feel here is a poet who knew what love is, while she sits afar off lonely and loveless. The love of the many she declares is a small thing in comparison with the love of one ; women fail here to generalize, too, as Romney might say.

But it is pitiful to cry so because you are hungry, and,

since every one must hunger for something, it is better to hunger for sweet companionship than for God's truth.

She passes on here to the consideration of the charge made against rhymers that they are envious, and repudiates the charge, for she does not envy the fine work of any of her contemporary poets, though she confesses to envying one because of his mother's love for him, and another because his wife loves him so much she forgets that he is celebrated. *Her* only loved ones are in heaven, and death sets a great barrier between the live and the dead, though there are people who have testified that spirits continue to feel the human way, and hate the unreasoning awe that waves them off from possible communion. She thinks this may be so !

Earth separates, too, as well as heaven. She has not seen Romney for two years, but has heard of his having divided Leigh Hall into almshouses.

It appears, here, that this very dismal and dissatisfied mood of Aurora's was a result of her having spent an evening at Lord Howe's and fallen in with Lady Waldemar, who was looking radiant. She overhears two men — one with a German student look and the other an Englishman, Sir Blaise Delorme — talking about Lady Waldemar's beauty.

The young man informs the other that she is soon to become the wife of their ablest man, Romney Leigh, and the conversation continuing, with one interruption from a third man objecting to Lady Waldemar's very low gown, reveals that the young man admires her greatly, while the older man is inclined to criticise. This brings out the fact that the young man has imbibed liberal notions in Germany which the older man decidedly objects to. The young man winds up by criticising Romney because he is a Christian Socialist instead of a full-fledged pagan socialist, and hints that in choosing Lady Waldemar Romney has converted her to his way of righteousness, and metamorphosed Venus Meretrix into a Blessed Virgin. The older man declares that one is either inside the church or outside it, implying that a Christian Socialist is an impossibility, and he is furthermore shocked at the blasphemy about the Blessed Virgin. The young man proceeds to prove his assertion about Lady Waldemar by telling how she has gone into Romney's work, and has even taken her turn at the washing-tub along with the poor girls at his new phalansteries.

Lord Howe comes up at this point, and entering into conversation with Aurora, tells her how he saw she felt sad and had kept a crowd of lion-hunters off. Then, sitting down beside her, he tells her he has a letter from a certain gentleman, John Eglinton, who makes him the bearer of love. But Aurora declares she cannot love, and refuses even to read the letter.

Lord Howe tries to persuade her to consider the matter, and realize that a happy life means prudent compromise, and that even for the sake of her art it would be better for her to improve her worldly circumstances. Aurora, with her high ideals as to the sacredness of her art, sorrowfully repels Lord Howe's arguments. As she is going across the room on Lord Howe's arm she meets Lady Waldemar, who in her ladylike manner proceeds to stab Aurora as cruelly as possible by talking to her of Romney and his work at Leigh Hall, hinting that she is thoroughly at home there, and asking if Marian, whom she is sure Romney never loved, has been quite lost sight of.

Aurora is helpless in her clutches and might have listened to her talk for an hour, answering yes, or no, if Lord Howe had not interposed, explaining that she was tired and wanted to say good night.

At home again, Aurora meditates upon the coming marriage of Lady Waldemar and Romney, concluding that, although Lady Waldemar had been so unkind, it was after all natural that she should hold her newly blossomed gladness in Aurora's face ; and that it was evident that Romney wanted a wife, and that since he never loved her nor Marian, she hopes he may truly love

Lady Waldemar, for good love ill placed is better than poor love given to one who deserves to be well loved. And if the worst is true and Romney is incapable of love, then Lady Waldemar is good enough for him. Then she decides that Lady Waldemar shall not have the satisfaction of thinking she has triumphed over her — writes her a note of congratulation, and bethinks her that in order to avoid the wedding she will go to Italy, and tells Lady Waldemar this in a postscript.

Here follow her preparations for a journey to Italy, in order to defray the expenses of which she is obliged to sell her choice books from her father's library.

Line 3. *Lava-lymph*: a daring expression, not to be taken in an exact sense but figuratively, for the molten liquid mass of chaotic matter fructifying into galaxies, that is, into clusters of worlds and planetary systems, under the imagined touch of creative power. "Lava" carries with it the idea of earthy matter in a fused state, "lymph" that of a limpid wateriness, — both in a condition of unusual potency, the first from volcanic force, the second from the sort of inspired possession associated with the word "lymph" in connection with Greek oracles. The Nymphs and Muses were goddesses of the fertilizing moisture of springs impregnated with exciting fumes, and this kind of "lymph" the poet has in mind here, supposing it to be in a susceptible state, feeling "God's finger."

29. *The primal rhythm Of that theurgic nature*: here again, as in preceding expressions (see foregoing note), the energy behind evolution, the pulse of a life-impetus imparted to matter at the moment of creation, is implied, "theurgic," derived from the Greek, meaning "God-stirred," or "God-enchanted."

75. "*Let no one be called happy till his death*" : from "Œdipus the King," of Sophocles, the closing lines, 1528–30.

87. *Like Atlas, in the sonnet*: Atlas, one of the Titans, was fabled to stand in the far west, bearing the world

upon his shoulders; hence the poet is here said to stand in the sonnet, like Atlas, because in that set brief form of verse he can sum up his meaning, as it were, in a condensed spherical shape, although he can only stand still there, this form not being favorable as the ballad-form is to movement.

Lines 96-99. *Stirred its bark With close-pressed bosoms . . . rivers garrulous With babble of gods:* compare with this poetic explanation of the origin of nature-myths the similar passage, " Never a senseless gust now man is born," etc., in Robert Browning's " Paracelsus." (See *Camberwell Browning*, Vol. i., part v., lines 718–732.)

113. *Panomphæan Joves:* the universal father or the God of the physical oracles of the universe, a Jove speaking through matter, " Panomphæan " being derived from the Greek πᾶν, all or Nature, and ὀμφή, oracle or divine voice. — *Fauns, Naiads, Tritons, Oreads:* minor semigods or male and female creatures of the woods and the water, respectively.

116. *Vampire-uses:* the vampire, according to mediæval superstition, was a dead creature maintaining a wandering existence on earth by sucking the blood of sleeping persons. Hence the comparison here is between the parasite life lent to natural objects by a mythology based on a physical conception of the universe, and the symbolic life lent to them by the spiritual conception of that universe of which the developed mind of the Christian poet should be capable.

139. *That epics have died out With Agamemnon and the goat-nursed gods:* Agamemnon being the leader of the Greeks in the expedition against Troy chronicled in Homer's epic of the " Iliad ; " and *the goat-nursed gods* being the gods of the Greek mythology, Zeus, the father of them, having been nursed by the goat, Almathea.

142-146. *Payne Knight, etc.:* Richard (1750–1824), English philologist, writer on Greek art and literature, member of Parliament, and trustee of the British Museum. In his " Prolegomena to Homer " he disputed Wolff's

conclusions (see note following on Wolff, book v., line
1246), and claimed that the Homeric poems were the work
of one man, but with interpolations by others, thus making
a specious semi-learned argument, as our poet detects.
Before the Parliamentary Committee of 1816, upon the
nation's acquisition of the Parthenon marbles, he gave
evidence against them, claiming that some of them were
Roman of Hadrian's time, and opposing the artist Haydon's testimony, so that, "out of delicacy to Mr. Payne
Knight," Haydon's evidence was dispensed with. He
told Lord Elgin that he had "lost his labor" in bringing the marbles over. The poet evidently took Haydon's
side of the question, and the opinion she held of Payne
Knight is figuratively implied in her curious parentheses,
wherein she says, virtually, that he was a *mountaineer*
or explorer upon the heights of art and mythology so ill-
fitted by nature for his task as often to reveal his imper-
fections. Hence, travelling *higher than he was born to
live*, he showed *the goitre in his throat* while he discoursed
of objects he saw but dimly. To contract goitre from
living on too high mountain peaks, and to be unable to
allow sufficiently for falsifying fog-effects, would be dis-
abilities of course in successful mountaineering. Aurora
sees the reality and humanness of Homer which Payne
Knight was not qualified to see.

Line 149. *Hector's infant whimpered at a plume* : alluding to one of Homer's natural touches. When Hector
would have taken his boy into his arms the babe clung
crying to his nurse, "scar'd at the dazzling helm and
nodding crest." (See "Iliad," Book vi., 595–601.)

156. (*Ask Carlyle*) : referring to Carlyle's "Heroes
and Hero Worship."

162. *Gaberdines* : a loose long outer coat.

169. *Mount Athos carved as Alexander schemed* : Di-
nocrates, the sculptor, is said to have suggested to Alexander the hewing of Mount Athos into the statue of a
conqueror with a city in his left hand, and in his right a
basin wherein all the waters of the region could be col-

lected, as in a reservoir, and thence water the pasture-lands below.

Line 207. *Roland with his knights at Roncesvalles :* Roland is the typical hero of feudalism, representing the utmost devotion to his liege, the Emperor Charlemagne, at the disastrous battle at Roncesvalles, as told in many ballad-cycles and especially in the " Chanson de Roland."

210. *King Arthur's self, etc. :* the hero of another cycle of mediæval ballads, familiar to modern English readers through Tennyson's " Idylls of the King," as Lady Guinevere, his wife, is also, and Camelot, his capital.

213. *As Fleet Street to our poets :* originally this read : " As Regent Street to poets." Mr. H. B. Forman, commenting on the change, considers that the sense is improved. Regent street being one of the finest streets in London, the original implication was that the poets would discern no romance in such a street of spruce shops and modern life. Fleet street has no pretensions, on the other hand, to elegance, and, besides being associated with the old debtor's prison, " the Fleet," formerly standing on it, it would seem sordidly modern to the poets from the fact that it is a centre for book-shops and newspaper and publishing offices.

240. *Jacob's white peeled rods :* this refers to Jacob's cunning arrangements with his father-in-law, Laban, by which, after they had agreed that all the streaked, speckled, and spotted flocks should be Jacob's share, he brought it about that the stronger of the flocks born should be streaked, speckled, and spotted. (See Genesis xxx., 37–43.)

250. *A wigless Hamlet :* referring to the effect of convention on the stage, which during the eighteenth century made it an established tradition that this part must be played in a wig, as was done by Garrick and Betterton. Kemble wore powder.

289. *King Saul's father's asses :* Saul, sent out to seek his father's asses, gave up hunting for them, when Samuel

met him and made him king, and thereafter he found the asses. (See I. Samuel ix. and x.)

Lines 292-299. *Weep, my Æschylus, etc.* : in the latter part of the life of this great Greek dramatist he was tried for an alleged profanation of the religious mysteries in his plays, and acquitted, but feeling strongly the indignity put upon him and the denseness of the Athenian public, he went to Sicily, where it is said that while meditating in the open fields he died from an eagle's dropping a tortoise in order to break its shell on his bald head, which the bird had taken for a stone. The poet, as she explains, reads the myth in her own way, to signify that the public of Athens virtually killed him, commissioning the bird, as it were, to crush his unprotected brain, which the poet, therefore, bids him cover and guard better, since it is clear that any merely lyric poet will be more readily heeded, the *Hyblan bee*, referring to the bee of Mount Hybla, famous for its honey, being here used by her as a figure for the accepted careless, poetic honey-sucker, concerned more for his own enjoyment than for human apprehension.

316. *Imogen :* the faithful, much-tried wife of Shakespeare's "Cymbeline." — *Juliet :* the fated girl-bride of his "Romeo and Juliet," in whom the world recognizes creatures of art made alive and human.

320. *The sacrificial goat for Bacchus slain, etc.* : a poetic picture of the ceremonies of the "dithyramb," or sacrificial hymn to Bacchus, the rude religious rite from which the Greek drama took its rise.

324-333. *The waxen mask, etc.* : in the description of this mask the *buskin* and the *mouth-piece*, the characteristics of the Greek stage, are brought out. The researches of modern archæologists are revising some of the earlier conjectures as to the construction and methods of the Greek theatre, but these more personal tools of the Greek actor are left unquestioned.

326. *Themis' son :* Prometheus, according to Æschylus, was the son of Themis, the personification of law in the sense of equity and order, and the source of foresight.

(See our poet's translation of the "Prometheus," Vol. VI. of this edition, lines 251–286.)

Lines 340–343. *Take for a worthier stage the soul itself, etc.*: by implication a characterization of what Robert Browning in his dramas and dramatic pieces attempted. "Instead of having recourse |to an external machinery . . . I have ventured to display somewhat minutely the mood itself in its rise and progress," he said in his preface to his early dramatic poem, "Paracelsus;" and again in his preface to his first play, "Strafford," he described it as "one of Action in Character, rather than Character in Action."

354. *That blue vein athrob on Mahomet's brow*: this is, perhaps, a fancy of the poet's upon the Mohammedan prophet's personal appearance. His beauty was delicate and unusual, according to all accounts we have consulted, but none of them include this trait.   *See Carlyle, H. and H. Worship*

361. *If Saint Preux Had written his own letters*: the lover of Julie in Rousseau's "Nouvelle Héloise," 1760, a love-romance told by him in letters supposed to be written by the lovers.

366. *Sorrowful great gift Conferred on poets, of a two-fold life*: compare with the expression of the poet of Robert Browning's "Pauline,"

> " I am made up of an intensest life,
> Of a most clear idea of consciousness
> Of self, distinct from all its qualities,
> From all affections, passions, feelings, powers."

(See *Camberwell Browning*, Vol. i., lines 268–271.)

400. *Pygmalion*: the Greek sculptor, who abhorred real women, and embodied in his marble the perfect woman of his dreams and fell in love with that, then, praying the goddess of love to make his statue alive, he had the joy of feeling his prayer granted. (See Ovid, Metamorphoses, x., also "Pygmalion and the Image," in William Morris's "Earthly Paradise.")

414. *Phœbus Apollo*: god of the sun and inspirer of

poets.   As Phœbus he represented the joy and life of
the sun, as Apollo its death-dealing power, — the darts
of Apollo, in Greek myth, meaning the arrows of Death.
So the poet speaks of this god as a soul within her soul,
both inspiring her and punishing her presumption, shoot-
ing down her works where they seem not to attain the
mark set by the inspiration of the attempt.

Line 477.   *Fame, indeed, 'twas said, means simply love* :
possibly this refers to Colombe's discovery, —

> " Nothing's what it calls itself.
>   Devotion, zeal, faith, loyalty, — mere love ! "

(See *Camberwell Browning*, Vol. iii., " Colombe's
Birthday," iv., 412.)

494.   *If Ugolino's full:* referring to Count Ugolino
described by Dante, " Inferno," xxxii., 125 ; xxxiii., 78.
He gnawed in ceaseless hatred the head of the man who
had imprisoned him and his sons together without food
until hunger forced him to devour their dead bodies.

505.   *Graham :* not an actual person, but any impres-
sionist artist whose vague means have power to convey
his impression.

509.   *Belmore :* a type of another artist in words who
through more minute and careful means keeps his aim in
mind and enforces it.

511.   *Mark Gage :* standing for the realist in expression
who through truth to the report the senses bring him of the
outer world brings out the light of the inner world,
wherefore, the poet says, *he leaves you with Plotinus.*

516.   *Plotinus :* (204–274) chief of the Neoplatonistic
philosophers who held that thought is made up of duality
— of essence and activity.   All ideas, therefore, are
spiritual forces whose sanction and origin transcend their
multitudinous results in all individual souls, but bring to
each all it can receive and understand of the Soul Universal, matter being the necessary tool of knowledge of the
transcendent unity.

Line 554. *Part as those at Babel :* who built the tower lest they be scattered (Genesis xi., 1–9), and thereby were struck with the sudden confusion of tongues which did scatter them, separating them widely as death separates.

556. *A living Cæsar would not dare to play, etc. :* suggested by the reverse side of Shakespeare's graveyard scene ("Hamlet," v., i., 202–239). Yorick and the games Hamlet had played with him in the flesh led him to moralize how

> " Imperious Cæsar dead and turn'd to clay
> Might stop a hole to keep the wind away,"

death debasing him, while our poet here brings out the awe striking a Cæsar in the presence of death.

559. *Sparrows five, etc. :* referring to Luke's version, xii., 6. Matthew x., 29, makes it two sparrows for one farthing. The reasoning drawn from this recalls Sludge's answer to the question, Shall God " stoop to such childish play "? (See " Mr. Sludge, ' The Medium,' " *Camberwell Browning*, Vol. v., 1074–1122.)

600. *Some Scandinavian myth of Lemures :* in the Roman mythology the Lemures were wandering spirits of the dead, somewhat like our ghosts. The meaning here seems to be not that the myth of Lemures is Scandinavian, but that some Scandinavian myth of such ghostly spirits as the Lemures, which conceives of them as godlike rather than merely horrible, as in the Roman myth, might have been the subject of Lord Howe's talk, judging from the way Lady Howe listened to his socialist theories.

632. *Thirty-five And mediæval :* our poet was one of the first to ridicule gently the faddishness of the nineteenth century revival of ecclesiasticism which, in 1856, the publication year of this poem, was a popular result of the Oxford Tractarian Movement, begun first by Dr. Pusey in 1833.

684. *Blessedest Saint Lucy :* the writers of the legend of Saint Lucy, mindful of the meaning of her name, derived from *lux*, light, tell how she plucked out her beauti-

ful eyes so as not to ensnare her lover and confuse the inward light which bade her devote herself to celibacy. She is represented by the church painters, accordingly, as bearing her eyes on a plate. The poet makes Sir Blaise propose that men follow Lucy's example, to avoid being tricked into choosing wives by the eyes' report of their good looks.

Line 730. *Pisgah-hill:* the hill whence Moses beheld the promised land. (Deuteronomy iii., 27.)

740. *Women-fishes:* meaning mermaids, of course, imagined to be half woman and half fish.

772. *Of Göttingen:* the student of the German University at Göttingen.

784. *Fourier:* François Charles (1772–1837), the French socialist, who advocated living in phalansteries coöperatively; frequently mentioned (see preceding Book ii., note, line 483, and Book ix., line 798).

798. *The statue called A Pallas in the Vatican:* this represents the goddess standing with a spear in one hand, a helmet on her head, and a snake coiled around her feet.

900. *Anne Blythe;* 902. *Pauline;* 905. *Baldinacci:* all imaginary stars of feminine genius, like Aurora, though in different lines of accomplishment.

911. *The holy ox on Memphis-highway:* the sacred bull, Apis, of the Egyptian religion was supposed to be the representative of the god Osiris, whose life had passed into that of the bull. In this shape, as Apis, the god was consulted at Memphis, and his oracle construed according to signs given by the bull, in seeming pleased or displeased. The poet imagines him here lowing with pleasure when sung to, like Aurora's public.

917. *A dropped star Makes bitter waters, etc. :* an allusion to the "star Wormwood" falling into the waters of the earth so that "men died of the waters because they were made bitter." (See Revelation viii., 10, 11.) The allusion is lightly applied to the embitterment of a wife of unusual talent dropped into domestic life, her powers cut off, thereby, from their natural artistic outlet.

Line 940. *Some golden tripod from the sea, etc.* : oracles
were founded usually, it is thought, in any special place,
because of some accidental discovery, taken to be of divine
origin, of some fetich stone, or some fissure in the earth
whence mephitic vapors arose and over which the prophetess sat on the sacred tripod, or three-footed stool, when
giving out her inspired oracles.   The latter was the
case at Delphi, the famous oracle of Apollo in Greece.
The practical necessity in a country like England for a
tripod, and one of gold at that, is here urged upon the
prophetess.

1096. *My woodland sister, sweet maid Marian* : an
allusion to the sweetheart of Robin Hood, the hero of the
mediæval ballads and stories of free forest life in England.

1197. *Nard* : an ointment prepared from the plant
spikenard, here imagined not to be of any use to a witch,
now, to grease her broomstick with, without gold in it.

1201. *It turns by sunset to a withered leaf* : in fairy
mythology this is generally what happened to all the gold
of fairies, witches, and conjurers.

1204. *Faustus* : the hero of the Faust legend was a
philosopher picked out by the devil, with God's consent,
to be tried by the possession of gold, as well as by love
and all prosperity.   (See Goethe's "Faust," Prologue.)

1205. "Leave my Job," *said God* : Job, like Faustus,
was tried, with God's consent, but by poverty and mis-
fortune instead of prosperity.   So are poets tried, thinks
Aurora.   (See the Book of Job.)

1218. *Elzevirs* : rare books, especially classics, highly
prized for their typographical beauty and scholarship,
published by the Elzevir family, in Amsterdam and
Leyden, about 1583–1680.

1222. *Conferenda hæc cum his* : compare this passage
with that.

1223. *Corruptè citat* : quoted incorrectly. — *Lege
potiùs* : read preferably.   All these refer to bits of com-
ment on the text written in the margin by her father

1226. *Twelve thrones up-piled* : the tribes of Israel

being twelve, it is supposed that this is supreme judgment dictated from as many thrones.

Line 1228. *Proclus :* a Byzantine Greek philosopher of the fifth century, whose books consist of commentaries on Plato and of philosophical writings seeking to prove the world eternal.

1246. *The kissing Judas, Wolff :* Frederick Augustus (1759–1824), German philologist, whose famous " Prolegomena ad Homerum " brought forward evidence that the " Iliad " and " Odyssey " of Homer, as now known to us, are made up of the work of various bards and rhapsodes of different epochs collected and adapted to the demands of a reading public. Aurora likens him to the *kissing Judas* because he seems to her to betray his master, Homer, while learnedly illustrating him, and therefore chooses to sell her folio Wolff instead of her Proclus.

1252. *Spondaic prodigious mouths :* referring to the broad, stately measure characteristic of Homer, the spondaic hexameter, or line of six feet with a spondee, or Greek foot of two long syllables in the fifth foot, wherefore she likens the line to wide mouths in the margins at the end of the lines, thus bringing up the ideas of both youth in poesy and of a large but simple eloquence.

Sixth Book. At the opening of this book Aurora has gone as far as Paris in her journey, and being in Paris takes occasion to express her opinion as to the French, whom she says the English have a scornful, insular way of calling light. On the contrary, she thinks them idealists, too absolute and earnest. They are moved by some general truth which, followed out, would lead to an ideal good, and, regardless of the distance nature places between thought and action, they rush upon impossible practice. Thus, though they constantly fall short of realizing their ideals, their earnestness and aspiration is sublime ; and even if all their dreams of a republic end in their having an emperor, he is no despot, but simply the head of the state, with all the people for a heart, so that autocratic rule in France may be said to be tempered by democracy.

She muses thus as she walks up and down the streets of Paris, which she describes in glowing colors, though not without a word of criticism against French art, which she describes as too absolute in its theories, like their social ideals, so that they do not sufficiently depict nature as it is.

The sight of the crowds causes her to ruminate further upon the importance of humanity to the artist. She would consider it weakness if she would not rather study an artisan's palm or a peasant's brow than confine herself to the observation of nature. Men of science and surgeons beat some artists in their appreciation of the value of humanity. In fine, the artist who seeks beauty only in delicate bits of nature is denied by nature the larger view of beauty which discovers it in the soul of the meanest among human beings, who in himself includes all nature. And if the artist needs humanity, it is equally true, as she goes on to remark, that humanity needs the artist perhaps more than he needs outside plans for his improvement.

At this point in her promenade she is startled by seeing among the crowd the face of Marian. The girl is lost again immediately, and Aurora, with frantic eagerness, tries to follow her up, but all to no purpose. The face eludes her, and disheartened, she returns to her home. She tries to interest herself in her plans for Italy, but the face of Marian haunts her, and she knows it could not have been a fancy, for she not only saw Marian's eyes, looking larger than they used to look and filled with a passionate despair, but she knows Marian's eyes saw her.

The question as to whether she will write and tell Romney troubles her, for if she does she will have to tell him the whole truth, that Marian clasped in her arms a child, of which fact Aurora takes the worst possible view, accusing Marian of being a wretch who has stolen a jewel she has no right to. What comfort will it give Romney, who is about to be married, that Marian is found, that she is not dead, but only damned ?

Aurora realizes here that she is jumping too quickly to conclusions in regard to Marian, decides she will not write to Romney and disturb his happiness, and, as for herself, that she must see Marian again. The police shall track her, and Marian shall be saved whether she will or no.

The police search for weeks, but to no purpose, and finally give it up, but Aurora cannot feel satisfied so ; and fortunately a happy chance brings her again face to face with Marian. Early one morning Aurora goes out to the flower market, and there she finds Marian, who is asking the price of a branch of flowering gorse, which she finds too much for her purse.

Aurora seizes Marian by the wrists, and when Marian tries to escape, declares she will not let go one whom she has sought for many days in her thoughts and prayers, and begs the poor girl to come with her and share her home, for she has a home for those two and no one else.

Marian shakes her head, saying that such a home would ill suit her, and thanking Aurora, who she says is as good as heaven itself, bids her " farewell." Aurora lets go Marian's hands, but asks for Romney's sake, to whom she had caused grief and reproach by her abandonment of him, that she will not thus say farewell. Marian is arrested by this, startled that any grief or reproach should have come to Romney because of her action, and asks how it is.

Aurora, not wishing to discuss these things in the open streets, authoritatively leads Marian off. They walk a mile in silence, when Marian asks if they have much farther to go, for there is one at home who needs her and whom she cannot let wait, not even to hear of Romney Leigh. Upon this Aurora says she will go with Marian. Marian with a spasm of anguish acquiesces, remarking that seeing will be better than hearing, and leads the way to her mean home — a room scarce larger than a grave and nearly as bare.

There she at once draws the covering off the child, a

beautiful boy asleep upon the bed. She shows for him such passionate devotion that Aurora feels called upon to moralize to Marian upon the subject of her wickedness in stealing this child from God. To which Marian retorts with warmth that she feels she has as sure a right to her child as any glad pure mother in the world, and that she did not steal him, but found him. She goes on to explain, in reply to Aurora's exclamation, that she found him in the gutter with her shame, and holds that when a girl has been treated with desperate cruelty, and a child comes to her, it is sent to her by God to make amends. She is worried now for fear the child will not like her since he has seen her grief and anguish. She composes herself again and smiles at the child, who laughs back at her and reassures her, and she triumphantly points out to Aurora that great and pure as she is, if she were even purer the child will always prefer his mother to her.

Aurora is not yet convinced, and continues to read Marian moral lessons, when Marian breaks out again, and at last makes it plain to Aurora that it was through no fault of hers that evil befell her, whereupon Aurora breaks down utterly, weeping, and embracing Marian, and swearing by the child that his mother shall be innocent before her conscience.

Marian is grateful that Aurora has cleared her from reproach, but she feels she is less than ever upon the level of Aurora's love since the world has treated her so badly ; that now she is as one dead, therefore she begs Aurora to leave her and let her rest. All that survives in her is the mother. She lives only for the child, and to prove that, she reminds Aurora that, though they have been talking there for half an hour, she has made no inquiries about Romney, for since she is dead it is nothing to her whether he be sick or sad.

Aurora instinctively feels that, in spite of this avowal, Marian would like to hear of Romney, so tells about him and tactfully leads up to the announcement of his engagement to Lady Waldemar, but Marian forestalls this

climax of the story, saying she expected it, for Romney
had loved Lady Waldemar so deeply.   Aurora is startled
by this turn of affairs and asks for light, and Marian,
after enjoining upon Aurora that she will never let Romney know of the dreadful trap she had fallen into, tells
her story.

She had loved Romney more as others pray, and had
sunk herself entirely in him, and supposed that his capacity for joy would be entirely filled up in doing good to
her, since doing good seemed so much his business.   But
gradually it dawned upon her that she would be out of
place in that Eden of delight, and that instead of making
him happy she would pull him down.   These thoughts
came to her through the insinuations of Lady Waldemar,
who, going to see Marian day after day, worked upon
her sensitive nature in such subtle ways that at last she
one day burst into tears and begged Lady Waldemar,
whom she thought wise and good, to tell her whether she
was doing right in marrying Romney.   Lady Waldemar,
with a great show of affection, told Marian the truths she
asked for : that Romney could not love her as men call
loving, though once wed he would treat her with the
utmost kindness and generosity ; that it was plain a man
like him needed a wife who would be on the same level
as himself ; and when Marian questions whether her devoted love will not raise her up, Lady Waldemar feared
that could not be ; and besides it was certain that Romney would suffer when his class turned the cold shoulder
on him for his shameful match.   Marian for an instant
doubts whether Romney would care for such things, but
Lady Waldemar cuts the doubt short by saying that one
so sensitive to the poor could not fail to be sensitive about
his own class, and finishes her work on Marian by con-
fessing that Romney had formerly loved *her*, Lady Waldemar.   But things had come in between them, and the
chance had passed.   Now she loved him, but he was
bound and an honorable man, and though Marian came
between her and heaven she loved Marian wholly.

Then Marian of course decided to give Romney up, and Lady Waldemar promised to provide the means for taking her out of England, which she did by putting her under the protection of one who had once been her waiting-maid, and who was going to Australia.

This woman turned out to be of the wickedest. Marian was not taken to Australia, but to Paris, to a shameful house where she was drugged and duped. After this she was mad for weeks, and, being let go by those who had trapped her, wandered up and down the country hunted by some prodigious dream fear at her back, until one day she came to herself and realized that there was a great red stone upon her sepulchre, which angels were too weak to roll away.

Line 69. *Carp at Cæsar for being bald:* the baldness of Cæsar is referred to sportively by the poet in her note on "To Flush, my Dog." (See Vol. III., page 369, of this edition.) Plutarch speaks of him as a small spare man with a delicate white skin. The allusion is to Napoleon III. here rather than to the Roman Cæsar, and is vague, not literal He also could be easily criticised on the outside like the Roman Cæsar, if no credit were given his soul or his motives.

70. *This Cæsar represents not reigns:* alluding to the plébiscite of the French which legally made him their emperor by eight million votes.

110. *The old Tuileries:* the palace of the French kings, in Paris, whimsically fancied here to be abashed at the new Empress Eugénie, who was not a member of any royal family, but not less beautiful than the queens whose reflections the mirrors of the Tuileries had, as it were, devoured.

129. *The first Napoleon's bones in his second grave, etc.:* alluding to the removal of his body from St. Helena where he had been buried to the mausoleum under the dome of the Hôtel des Invalides, in Paris. (See "Buried and Crowned," and notes thereon, in Vol. III. of this edition.)

Line 132. *Louis Philippe:* (1773–1850) king of the French from 1830–1848, when he was driven away by the revolution of 1848, following shortly upon the celebration in Paris of the return of the ashes of Napoleon I., and succeeded by the dominance of Napoleon III.

166. *Nilus:* the Latin name for the Nile, the sacred river of Egypt, whose sources were long unknown, and but recently by Livingstone and Stanley explored.

167. *Changes of the moon Among the mountain peaks of Thessaly:* the earliest European astronomical observations were made by the Greek astronomer Aratus, in the Thessalian mountains, and there too the myth of Endymion, the beloved of the moon-goddess, is placed.

169. *Magic crystal:* the ball of glass used by seers in divining mysteries of the future is here likened to the moon. All such beautiful objects of Nature are affirmed to be less fruitful to observe than the ugliest parts and properties of human nature.

214. *Washing seven times* : an echo of Naaman's cure for his leprosy by bathing seven times in the Jordan. (See II. Kings v., 1–14.)

264. *The Institute:* the Institut de France, made up of five academies : the Académie Française, for literature proper, the Académie des Inscriptions et Belles Lettres, des Beaux Arts, des Sciences, des Sciences Morales et Politique. It was a creation of the French Revolution, starting from an idea of Fontenelle, and M. Colbert originally intended it to become a universal academy of all literatures. The law incorporating it was passed in the last days of the convention, Oct. 25, 1795. The conception of a purely literary academy properly belongs to Madame de Staël. Napoleon I. especially fostered the Institute.

273. *Dumas:* Alexandre Dumas *fils* (1824–1897) is probably meant. He inherited much of the genius of his father, the author of "Monte Cristo," but was of sterner mould and a more orderly mind. His dramas were marked by themes and methods which aroused con-

troversy and made the honor of his membership in the
Institute difficult.

Line 808. *Madrepores :* a genus of coral-building animals
in which the calcareous axis has a surface beset with
minute starry and branching-out depressions.   The name
is derived from the French *marbré*, "spotted," and
pore, indicating this spotted porous look.   The term
seems to be used here descriptively and not with scientific
exactness.

Seventh Book.   Marian goes on with her story in this
book.   She is taken in by a miller's wife, who treats her
kindly and finds a place for her in Paris.   Her Paris
mistress is easy with her, not through kindness, but because she leads an easy life herself, between her looking-
glass and her lover.   But there came a time when from
Marian's appearance her mistress concluded that she was
no reputable girl, and Marian, for the first time aroused
to the consciousness of what was impending, could only
tell the truth as to the wrong she had experienced, and
her mistress, entirely unsympathetic, dismissed her at
once.   Marian is not surprised that she is indifferent as
to what becomes of *her*, but is surprised that she should
have taken no thought of what might become of the child,
and Aurora wonders at the uncompromising attitude of
a woman who has scandals of her own, and she sharply
denounces the thrifty vice of these light women, declaring she would rather meet with the worst sort of women
than touch one of these with her finger.   Marian finally
found a place with a kindly sempstress, and has thus been
enabled to live for her child.

Aurora now proposes that Marian and the child shall
go with her to Italy, and as the child is half an orphan it
shall have two mothers and they will live together.
Marian's only reply is to hold up the child for Aurora to
kiss, so showing her trust and aquiescence.

And thus Aurora thinks she will pay Romney's debts.

She is confronted again with the problem as to whether
she will write and tell him Marian's story, but hesitates

to make his life miserable by exposing the perfidy of
Lady Waldemar. Then she thinks how strange it was
that while Marian was telling her story she heard constantly the voice of one who years ago had said to *her*,
" Be my wife," and she thinks how she might have
saved him, and at last confesses to her own heart that she
loves him, though she is in the mood to struggle against
the feeling, and, as if there were a man within her, de-
spises her own tears and weakness, and tries to make
excuses to herself for them on the score that it is only
pity for Romney's fate in falling into the hands of Lady
Waldemar that has moved her so deeply.

She clears the atmosphere, however, with her tears, and
decides that the man within her shall act, and that she will
write plain words to England, whether it is too late or not.
She thereupon writes to Lord Howe enclosing the story
as Marian had told it, and requesting him to tell Romney
all if he is not yet married ; but if he is married simply
to tell him Marian is found and is to live in future
with Aurora.

She goes on, with a touch of sarcasm, to say it will
make him merry in his love, and to express some wonder
at the quickness with which men forget the passionate
events of their lives.

Then she writes a bitter, scornful letter to Lady Waldemar, in which she denounces her outrageous action in
regard to Marian, tells her of Marian's child, and warns
her to beware how she acts toward Romney in their
married life, for as long as she fulfils her duties toward
him Marian and herself will be silent, but if ever Romney
is wounded or ill-content or tormented in his house, they
will speak, and such a noise will follow, more dreadful
than the last trump's, that Romney will push her forth as
none of his.

Aurora feels relieved after having wept her tears and
expressed her opinions, and goes into the next room to
look at Marian and her babe, who are lying there asleep.
She feels herself humbled in the presence of their inno-

cence, and would fain get leave to creep in somewhere
"within this round of sequestration white."

The next morning they start for Italy, and Aurora
describes how all through the journey she imagined she
heard Romney's wedding-bells, and how she felt weak and
almost lost consciousness, but somehow recovered herself
when she caught Marian's eyes, because she realized how
much Marian needed her to be strong.

She describes in vivid symbols their arrival in the
station at Marseilles, where they took the boat and spent
the night on the water ; and Marian slept, but she, not
able to sleep, mounted guard over the others.   She still
hears the marriage-bells afar off sounding as some child's
go-cart might to a dying man.   She sits silent, and so sad
she would have been willing to die at that time.   And
now they begin to draw near Italy, which she describes in
a series of beautiful word-pictures.

Aurora's first thought when she sees Italy is not of
that, but of her father and his house without him, which
brings to her mind how much the charm of nature de-
pends upon the human associations connected with it,
and when they are broken the same scene hurts instead of
delights.   Marian, noticing how melancholy Aurora
looks, leaves the child and comes over to speak to her
and comfort her, for which kind thoughtfulness Aurora
gives thanks.

Arrived in Florence, Aurora takes a house with a beautiful view.

After many weeks had passed without any word from
England she at last receives a letter from Vincent Carrington, who tells her of the success of her new book, in
which she seems to have convinced the critics that a
woman can write something worth while, and of his own
admiration of it ; also that he is about to marry Kate
Ward, whom he hopes she will love.   He tells how her
topaz eyes haunted him until he painted them and turned
them against the wall, and now he has painted the whole
face, having given up his mythological subjects.   Kate

Ward, he declares, knows all Aurora's books by heart and quotes them against him. She insisted on having Aurora's last book painted in her hands, as well as upon wearing a cloak like one Aurora once had. He wonders whether Aurora will be as surprised at his marriage as Romney was, who stammered out a word or two when he heard it and was then silent. Carrington goes on to say Leigh has changed, and that he has not spoken of this because "conscious of her (Aurora's) heart," and he feels how poor it would be simply to say he is sorry. He had hoped Romney and she might have come together, but they seemed to have gotten farther and farther apart until this happened. When Romney took the fever he had been told that Lady Waldemar waited upon him like any common nurse, and Lord Howe had been a trump too ; but still a man like Leigh may lose. He ends his letter with a few light remarks.

Aurora comes to the conclusion upon reading this letter that Romney is married and that is the reason Vincent is so sorry. She thinks it was natural that Lady Waldemar nursed him, and that Vincent, himself being in love, should admire her for it ; at the same time he says at the last, " I'm sorry." So Vincent as well as she does not think Lady Waldemar a good wife for Romney. Vincent's remarks about being " conscious of her heart," etc., ruffle her, though she says they do not, and she suddenly feels stifled and throws open the blinds in spite of the hot sun, and at last realizes that books may succeed and at the same time lives fail. But in the midst of her mood of self-despisal she recovers herself and decides that she will be meek and learn to reverence even herself.

She remarks that Vincent calls her book good and she "a woman," which once had made her laugh, but now she feels so keenly her womanhood, she cares little about compliments on writing good books.

She goes on, however, to talk about her book and lay down various principles of art. She feels she has written

truth in her book, for truth belongs neither to man nor
woman, but to God.   The truth which she has enunci-
ated is the indivisibility of the spiritual and the natural.
Without the spiritual, the natural is impossible, — no form,
no motion ; without the sensuous, the spiritual is inappreciable, — no beauty or power.   She enlarges upon this
thought, presenting it from many points of view, and
finally sums up by saying that if we say a true word we
feel at once it is God's and pass it on ; that the end of
woman or of man is not a book, which at best is but a
word in art, and soon grows cramped with years.   Art
being the larger, life must feel the soul and live past it,
for more is felt than is perceived, more perceived than
can be interpreted, and love strikes higher than art can
ever reach, and when at last we are satisfied we do not
call it truth, but love.

She decides here to shut the blinds, as she has not so
much of her mother's blood in her that she can stand the
boiling sun, remarks upon the inadequacy of a life that is
not pieced with another life, and prepares to write a word
of congratulation to Kate and Carrington.   If it were
not for Romney she should be glad, certainly she would
have been glad if he had married Kate.

She now describes her life in Italy with Marian and
the child, and is sure she ought to be glad, if it were not
for Romney.   She dwells upon Romney and his affairs
again, once more emerging from her thoughts upon him
by praying to be sustained, and that no life, not even her
own, shall seem intolerable.

Taking up her life in Italy, she finds it different now
that the innocence of her childhood is gone, though she
seeks the same pleasures in nature, but all nature's creatures seem farther off, as if a gulf were fixed between
them.

She goes once to the little mountain-house where she
used to live with her father, but finds it so changed she
can never go back, nor can she after this shock visit either
her father's or her mother's graves.   Assunta is dead,

too, and she finds herself entirely solitary and alone in this land of strangers, and would really be glad of this if she could become as foreign to herself as she is to others.

She passes many evenings wandering up and down in the crowd, observing them and imagining their lives, or watching the sunsets from the bridge, or attending vigils in the church.   One evening she saw Sir Blaise Delorme in the Santissimo.   He saw her, but only half bowed, for she slipped behind a pillar.   In England they were hardly acquaintances, but seeing him has disturbed her life, and after that she does not go out so much, but sits at home for the most part, musing.

Line 10.   *A motherly, right damnable good turn* : in the first edition this read, "A motherly, unmerciful good turn."   It has been objected that this is more characteristic of Marian, the present reading being what Mrs. Browning thought about it.   Marian herself, feeling the bitter pinch of it, might have flared out with the unequivocal word.

147.   *Lamia:* a mythical woman monster externally enchanting, but serpentine and revolting when unmasked. (See Keats' "Lamia.")

226.   *Cervantes:* Miguel (1547–1616), the Spanish novelist, whose famous romance of "Don Quixote" here referred to depicts in his Don one of the last of the knights of romantic chivalry, and who, the poet asserts, if he had possessed Shakespeare's sympathy with the woman nature would have painted a feminine Don Quixote.

300.   *Gambled deep As Lucifer, and won the morning star:* a double allusion.   The chief of the fallen angels was the spirit of the Morning Star, according to tradition, the name Lucifer signifying light-bringer, and he being the son of Zeus and Aurora in Greek mythology.   Casting everything upon success in tempting Adam and Eve in Eden, he lost through their redemption, and his title of Morning Star was borne thenceforth by Christ, as in Revelation viii., 10.   Mrs. Browning makes poetic use of the transposed symbolism in her "Drama of Exile."

(See Vol. II. of this edition, also notes on same, lines
149 and 2230.)   Here the allusion is to Lady Waldemar as
Lucifer, and to her success, and the good Romney is
spoken of as the Morning Star and as her prize.

Lines 342-3.   *For which inheritance . . . you sold that
poisonous porridge:* referring to Esau's selling his birthright to Jacob for a mess of pottage.   (See Genesis xxv.,
29–34.)

350.   ' *Ye shall not yoke together ox and ass* ' : " Thou
shalt not plow with an ox and an ass together." (Deuteronomy xxii., 10.)

418.   *Dijon:*   one hundred and ninety-seven miles southeast of Paris in the Coté d'Or province, a city of special
interest to the Brownings because it was the family home
of their friend, the French critic Milsand, the Maison
Milsand being one of the show places of the ancient town.
— *Lyons:* directly south of Dijon on the Rhone river.
The description of the journey past these cities and on to
Marseilles (see lines 449-452) on the French sea-coast, and
thence to Genoa across the boundary-line in Italy (lines
484-489), is of interest as described here because a route
familiar in the poet's own journeying to Italy through
France.

432.   *Thor-hammers:*   Thor, son of the Norse god
Odin, was the thunderer and god of strength and wielded
an irresistible hammer that could cleave rock like the tun-
nelling tools of modern human engineers.

470.   *Dull Odyssean ghosts:* an allusion to the lifeless
phantoms of the under world thronging eagerly about
Ulysses to drink the blood of his sacrificed animal life and
so get vigor enough to talk to him who had come over
the seas to them from the upper earth, as told in the
" Odyssey," Book xi.

516.   *Bellosguardo:* in the outskirts of Florence, in
Tuscany, commanding the wide prospect described.   Here
two especial friends of Mrs. Browning's had villas —
Mr. Lytton, son of Bulwer-Lytton, the novelist, and
Miss Isa Blagden.   Referring to Miss Blagden's in a

letter to Mrs. Jameson, the poet adds the caution in parenthesis, " (not exactly Aurora Leigh's, mind).''

Line 519. *Fiesole*: a hillside town on the Arno, three miles above Florence.

520. *Mount Morello*: the highest of the Apennines, northwest of Florence.

521. *The Vallombrosan mountains*: where the famous monastery and pine-woods of Vallombrosa are, now an afternoon's journey from Florence.

566. *Od-force of German Reichenbach*: Carl von (1788 ——), chemist, discoverer of paraffin (1831) and creosote (1833), and establisher of extensive factories in Moravia whence he derived a fortune, and the discoverer also of an alleged imponderable force in nature called by him " od,'' which he describes in several works upon it as analogous to electric and magnetic force and as widely diffused. He attributed to it the likes and dislikes of men, and affirmed that it was seen, but only by the *sensitive*, in the form of an undulating light.

586. *Danaës*: Danaë, daughter of King Acrisius, according to the oracles, would have a son who would cause his grandfather's death, so she was shut up in an underground prison where none might behold her, but Zeus saw her, loved her, and wooed her in a shower of gold. This myth had inspired Carrington for two canvases, one ideal, with Kate Ward's eyes, the second frankly all herself.

662. *Persiani*: an Italian plural for the Persian or Venetian blinds or curtains made of slats, strung parallelwise across the window, and common in Italy.

663. *Love and Psyche*: a favorite piece of statuary representing the god of love, Eros or Cupid, and his love, Psyche, the impersonation of the soul or immortal life.

679. *Nepenthe*: or nepenthes, Egyptian opiate, said to banish sorrow, the name being derived from the Greek νη, not, and πένθος, grief.

746. *Our Phædons*: that is, our arguments upon life and death and the soul, like the " Phædo '' of the

"Dialogues of Plato," which narrates the last scene in the life of Socrates and the discussion with his friends on the highest themes until he drank the poison, as he was condemned to do, and died.

Line 786. *Antinous :* a beautiful youth, the favorite of the Emperor Adrian, whose portrait busts are among the treasures of Roman art.

805-6. *Cup, column, or candlestick . . . patterns of what shall be in the Mount :* alluding to the instructions given Moses for the construction of the Tabernacle, and every minutest utensil and detail of it, according to patterns shown him by Jehovah on Mount Sinai. (See Exodus xxv–xxxi.)

810. *Said a poet of our day :* Robert Browning. (See "Pippa Passes," Introduction, lines 190–201.)

822. *Bush afire with God :* Exodus iii., 2–5.

830. *As Jove did Io :* the god turned Io, the granddaughter of the god Oceanus, into a heifer, stung by a gad-fly and driven over the deserts of the world, as told by Æschylus in his "Prometheus." (See Mrs. Browning's translation in Vol. VI. of this edition.)

887. *Digamma :* the name for the Greek letter double gamma, or gamma repeated, which was early disused, and its function in the Greek alphabet and language obscured, dropped *down some cranny,* therefore, *beyond the critic's reaching.*

902. *Medæan boil-pot :* the sorceress Medea brewed in her pot a concoction made up of all manner of animal and vegetable life, — as the witches of "Macbeth" did in imitation of this Greek witch, — singing incantations over it, till the bubbling mixture was able to restore the youth of the aged Æson, father of her husband, Jason. (See Ovid, Metamorphoses, vii.)

917. *Samminiato :* a surburban hill southeast of Florence, where the church of the same name stands, a Tuscan Romanesque structure of the twelfth century.

921. *Persiani :* see preceding note, line 662.

935. *Dante's purple lilies :* referring to the purple blos-

soms swelling out upon the bare tree of the earthly Paradise to which Beatrice in the griffin-drawn car led Dante,
in the vision of the mystical procession, described in
Cantos xxix.–xxxiii. of the "Purgatorio." The elabora-
tion of the meaning of the symbol seems to be meant by
his blowing the lilies *to a larger bubble with his prophet
breath*.

Line 942. *Ichor:* the blood that flowed in the veins of
the gods was not like human blood, but a colorless fiery
liquid called ichor.

969. *A trick of ritournelle:* a way of repeating the burden, returning to the theme, either in the verses or music,
so called from the Italian *ritornare*, to return; in *ritournelle*, the diminutive form signifies a "little *return*."

986. *Alaric:* the Visigoth king of the fifth century,
whose devoted warriors turned aside the course of the
river Busento in Southern Italy and buried him there in
the river-bed with the richest treasures, afterwards slaying
the grave-diggers and returning the waters over him that
none might disturb his tomb.

1021. *Auto-vestments:* garments to be burned in at an
auto-da-fě, or "act of faith," as the word means, the fiery
trial of heretics and unbelievers, especially held in Spain,
but familiar in Florence too.

1095. *Grillino:* the Italian name for a cricket.

1115. *Valdarno:* the valley of the Arno river,

1124. *Lingots:* same as "ingot," or "linget,"a mass
of gold or other metal in the shape in which it was melted
in the mould.

1176. *And* issimo *and* ino *and sweet poise Of vowels:* referring to the musical Italian inflections for the super-
lative and comparative degrees.

1181. *Donay's:* a favorite Florentine café in the Via
Tornabuoni, which has a branch in the Florentine Park,
the Cascine.

1198. *Grasshoppers at Athens:* an allusion to the
Athenian tradition that they were a race sprung from
grasshoppers.

Line 1256. *Benigna sis :* be thou blessèd !

1262. *He heareth the young ravens :* Psalms cxlvii., 9.

Eighth Book. At the opening of this book Aurora is sitting upon her terrace, with a book, though she is not reading it, while Marian is in the garden below peeling a fig for the child. Marian laughs, and glances above with shame that Aurora should have heard her. Aurora thinks, however, that she has the right to laugh, for God himself is for her, while for Aurora there is somewhat less.

The shadows of the evening creep on, fill the valley, and drown the city as in an enchanted sea, the Duomo bell strikes ten, the gas-lights begin to appear, when suddenly Romney stands before her. She rises and then sits down perturbed, and finally stammers out, "You, Romney ! — Lady Waldemar is here ? "

Romney answers, in a voice not his own, that he has a letter from Lady Waldemar, which she may read presently, but he must be heard first, for he has travelled far to speak to her. Aurora trembles as he touches her, and motions him to a chair, but he sits down slowly on the couch beside her. Aurora remarks that it is wonderful he has come, as wonderful as the stars above to which she points. In reply he murmurs, "Then you do not know." But she replies she knows, having had the news from Vincent Carrington. She is rather surprised that he should leave his work, but supposes he will make a work-day of his holiday.

He asks if she has Vincent's personal news, to which Aurora replies she has, and that all that ruined world of his seems crumbling into marriage, and that Carrington has chosen wisely. Romney seems to be surprised that she regards this marriage so favorably, and mutters some incoherences which make Aurora think that now he has married Lady Waldemar, like a man he loves Kate Ward, and she says to Romney she did not think he knew Kate Ward. Romney replies he never had known her, with some further remark upon her topaz eyes, which Au-

rora again misinterprets. It then comes out that Aurora
had never received a letter from Lord Howe which was sent
in charge of Sir Blaise Delorme. Romney thinks Aurora
would have been less startled to see him if she had read that
letter, for there were facts to tell that needed to be told
gently.   Aurora, still misunderstanding, supposes he
thought it necessary to break gently to her the news of
his marriage to Lady Waldemar. She tells him it is not
usual with him to prepare the way for his coming like a
Greek king coming from Troy with three-piled carpet, and
though he has come without preparation she can stand it.
She is sorry to lose Lord Howe's gossipy letter, as it is
rather dull there, but as a preparation for Romney's coming it was unnecessary. It was nothing for her to start
when she saw him — she had started at a cock-chafer the
night before and shook for half-an-hour. It's a woman's
way, and he should have learnt enough of women by this
time not to conclude that such things mean the winter's
bitter, but that the summer's sweet. He hopes the summer
may ever be green with her, though he remarks upon
her bitterness to her sex and her coldness.   Still he is
content. She can bear his sudden step beside her, but
he would be greatly moved if he heard her voice soften
unaware in pity of his condition.

Aurora thinks him indeed pitiable as the husband of
Lady Waldemar, but speaks to him calmly to the effect
that though what we choose may not in itself be good,
yet, in so far as it is chosen by us, makes it good for us.

He inquires now how Marian is, and learns she is well
and there, but expresses a wish to speak with Aurora
alone before he sees Marian.

Then he tells her how he has read her new book, and
how it has become part of his being ; and when Aurora
waives his compliments, and beseeches him to wish some
happier fortune to a friend than even to have written a
much better book, he answers gently that of course the
poet looks beyond the book he has made, but for him
who did not make it it is another thing, and this special

book draws him up above himself, by which he means no compliment. He will not even say that richer, fuller books might not be written, but that this book has made its special appeal to him and has won his soul.

Aurora finds it sad that his appreciation comes so late. If he had spoken with such sympathy many years ago it would have pleased her more as a hope than it can at all as a grace. To which he replies, " Ay, 'tis night."

Aurora catching at this, proposes they look at the stars instead of talking about books. In reply he addresses her with such passionate utterance that she breaks in, telling him he is speaking wildly, reminding him that they have grown old and cold, and regretting that she recalled the incident of her birthday ten years back. He goes on, however, in the same vein and confesses that he has found out at last that upon that birthday morning it was Aurora who was right, while he was wrong. He points out, at some length, how he has failed, Aurora interrupting him from time to time by saying, "Speak wisely, cousin Leigh."

He ends by saying he yields, that Aurora has conquered, but Aurora confesses that she has failed also, and talks in such a melancholy strain that Romney exclaims passionately that she could scarcely have been sadder as his wife. Aurora intimates to him here that he is going too far, and when he declares she misunderstands him, she says she is glad, and begs him to keep from misconceptions too, and declares she isn't so very sad after all, and what sadness she has comes of her being older and wiser, and, furthermore, she was in the main right on that birthday morning, as she proceeds to show. She concludes that though they two have failed, God never fails, and that they should be ashamed to sit beneath the stars, impatient at being nothing.

Romney thinks that if he could sit thus with her forever his failure would seem better than success. He speaks again of her book and the effect it had had upon him. Others of her poems had moved him, but he had always seen her in them ; this, however, was separable from herself, and it had brought home to him the truth of the interdependence of the natural and spiritual life as nothing had ever done before, and made him realize his own mistake in emphasizing the material side of life in his reforms, and even the mistakes of many Christian teachers who separate the natural life too much from the spiritual. After he has enlarged upon these thoughts, Aurora asks him if he has now more hopes of men, to which he replies that he has come to believe that God will do his work, and there is no need to be disturbed when Romneys or others fail with their quack nostrums.

Aurora thinks it well not to lean too dangerously the other way, for she is sure that no earnest work fails so much that it is not at least a grain of sand in the sum of human action, to which Romney agrees, and adding illustrations to the thought carries it a little farther to the effect that not only is it impossible for one man to reform the world, but perhaps it would not be well to abolish evil, since through evil, which God permits, man develops his free will. In fact, he is just as much in love with an imperfect world now as he was once in love with a perfect one, and is so sarcastic about his old schemes, where virtue is dealt out gratuitously with the soup at six, etc., that Aurora begs him to treat himself with more respect.

They continue their talk in the same vein, both agreeing that there is too much theorizing over the evils of society as well as over their remedies, and Aurora declaring that the trouble, too, with women is that they talk too much of woman's mission, woman's rights, and so on, instead of doing. As soon as they show they can do artist-work men will recognize them. Romney declares it is the mood of the age to boast and do not, and reiterates his conviction that society cannot be made over again according to a set pattern, because it must be the outcome of the development of its members, just as genuine government is the expression of a nation.

Aurora finding him so sad asks him if all his work at Leigh Hall has come to nought.

Romney explains that it *was* nought, for he could not get his men and women of disorderly lives suddenly to begin living orderly lives. The church objected to his trying to do good without its help, the Vicar preached against him. He had his windows broken, he was shot at, and finally the discontent of the people he was trying to benefit grew so great, because they were not allowed to be as evil as they had been, that they set fire to Leigh Hall and burned it. Upon Aurora's expression of surprise, Romney remarks that Vincent's news must have come rather stinted, and he seems surprised by the fact that Aurora is sorry. He goes on with a vivid description of the fire, telling how even the poor people he had housed clapped their hands at the blaze, and how he himself, when he saw the flames, realized that they were saving the people from his saving, and making a pretty show besides, which was the best he had ever done, and he himself almost felt like clapping. When the whole house finally collapsed in a heap of ruins, he felt like a Leigh for a moment or two; then he immediately turned his thoughts to the houseless wretches.

Aurora's sympathy overcomes him, and he asks her if she will not go and see the ruins, for they would be worth a poet's seeing. She does not answer, because she questions whether she has a right to weep with Romney since a woman stands between his soul and hers. At last she breaks the silence by asking if he were ill afterwards.

He replies that he was ill and hoped to die, but failed as he had failed to live, and so grew willing, as he had tried all ways, just to try God's way now.

He goes on from this to show that when one has once sinned, the sin itself colors one's very virtues afterwards, as in his case, for he had intended marrying where he did not love, and now it has become his duty to marry where he does not love.

In the talk that follows he refers to his duty to Marian,

and lets Aurora know that his love for her is so great that he will not be able to stand seeing her in the same house with some one else called his wife.

Aurora feels surprised and somewhat offended that Romney should address her in this way, answers rather coolly, indicating that she thinks Romney has gone too far, and finally ends up by assuring him that she will never have any wish to enter the house where Lady Waldemar is mistress.

Romney breaks out passionately at this, and Aurora at last learns he has not married Lady Waldemar, while Romney declares that in supposing he could marry Lady Waldemar Aurora has wronged his soul more than any who have maligned his motives or burned his house. Then he gives her the letter to herself from Lady Waldemar.

Line 21. *Boccaccio's tale, The Falcon :* the story of Sir Federigo, the ninth tale, told on the fifth day in Boccaccio's "Decameron," retold by Longfellow among his "Tales of the Wayside Inn," and by Tennyson in "The Falcon."

32. *Cue-owls :* the owl's cry gives it its common name in Italy.   From the joint evidence of Mrs. Browning here and Mr. Browning in "Andrea del Sarto," line 210, it appears the sound of *oo* is noticeable in the Florentine *àulo*, which is probably the *Bubo* of the same family as our cat-owl.

33. *The Poggio :* a fine avenue of oaks and cypresses leading out from the Porta Romana or Roman Gate of Florence.

44. *Duomo-bell :* the bell of the Duomo or Cathedral of Santa Maria del Fiore in Florence.

49. *The Pitti's Palace front :* the Pitti Palace erected in 1440, one of the most beautiful of the Renaissance palaces in Florence, now an official residence of the King of Italy.

50. *Maria Novella Place :* where the Dominican church of Santa Maria Novella stands.

Line 54. *Buonarroti's bride*: the Duomo, or Cathedral church of Santa Maria del Fiore, begun by Arnulfo in 1296, and finished by Brunelleschi in 1426, whose dome especially was so much admired by Michael Angelo Buonarroti that he said "it could be varied, but not improved, no !" and that he would make its sister for St. Peter's in Rome "a little bigger, but not more beautiful."

151. *Pauls*: Italian silver coins worth ten cents, here used as a synonym for money in general, as if one should say, "Because of shillings and pence."

185. *Chianti*: a light wine, the common product of the Italian vineyards.

388. *Phalarian bull*: Phalaris, a tyrant of Agrigentum, of the fifth century before Christ, who used to torture his subjects, had a bull of brass made which he used as a torture chamber.

507. *Ulysses' dog knew him*: the aged dog Argus pricked up his ears at the approach of his disguised master, and wagged his tail where he lay neglected at the stable door. (See "Odyssey," Book xvii.)

769. *Whatever may be lacking on the Mount*: on Mount Sinai, where the patterns for the Tabernacle were given to Moses. (See preceding book, notes 805–6.)

795. *When the prophet beats the ass The angel intercedes*: referring to Balaam's beating his ass when it saw the angel before its master did and refused to go on. (See Numbers xxii., 21–34.)

850. *A Cyclops' finger*: that is, the finger of a giant, the Cyclopes being sons of Cœlus and Terra, or sky and earth.

984. *'Vale et plaude'*: "farewell and be praised," the good-by and applause grimly blended by the Romans when the gladiator was to die in the fight that distinguished him.

1008. *Like brute Druid gods*: called "brute" here because they demanded human sacrifices.

1020. *Who had burnt the viol*: an allusion, perhaps,

to the desolation prophesied by Amos upon the Israelites when their viol-playing was to be interrupted by the burning of their house. (See Amos vi.) Aurora's response is to the effect that after the burning of the viol one does not return to the cruder music of the cymbals of careless joy.

Line 1113. *Metaphrase :* a rejoinder phrase capping the other, like the paired phrases of the short dialogue between the characters of the Greek drama.

1136. *Their cup at supper . . . they Give at cross-time on a sponge, etc. :* alluding to the wine with which Christ's cup was filled at the Last Supper, in contrast with the sponge wet in vinegar and gall reached up to him at his crucifixion. (Luke xxii., 11–18 ; John xix., 29.)

1144. *Moses' bulrush boat :* in which his mother launched him on the river in hopes to save him. (See Exodus ii., 3–10.)

Ninth Book. This book opens with Lady Waldemar's letter to Aurora, of which she has in a spirit of vindictiveness made Romney the bearer, choosing that Aurora shall have it ratified from Romney's mouth that she has been foully wronged. After all, she says, she thanks Aurora for proving there are some things she could not do even to save her life or for the love of Romney. She regrets she had once shown her heart to Aurora, who also had a sort of heart and herself loved Romney. She describes how she found out when she nursed Romney through his fever that he loved Aurora, and how Romney requested her to read Aurora's book to him, which she did, and closed the reading and her attentions to Mr. Leigh by remarking that she hated a woman who does better than to love, and that such a woman will never do anything very well, and that she preferred male poets.

The next time she saw Romney, Lady Waldemar continues, he and Lord Howe called, and she had read Aurora's letter. When they referred to her part in the transaction in regard to Marian, she asked pardon for having done no better than to love, and told them how she had taken some trouble for Romney's sake because she knew he did not love the girl, how she had entrusted Marian to her own maid, who had once lived with her five months, with a lavish purse to carry her to Australia where she had a husband. She is sorry if the maid lied, and she would rather have mended the poor child's silly head with gold than have it crushed with so much wrong.

Romney, however, had repelled the idea of any help from Lady Waldemar for his wife, as he henceforth called Marian, whom he tells her he is going to Florence to claim. For the rest Howe and Romney were glad to acquit her of the heaviest charge.

So they parted, and face, love, and voice were wiped out, and she concludes she has been too human, that people of her rank have no business with any blood in their veins. When the game to adore is played in vain, however, they can play on at leisure at being adored. Smith is already swearing at her feet, but she will have none of him, for he is too much of a socialist like Romney. She offers Smith to Aurora, who she says will want some comfort when the marriage between the unspotted Erle and the noble Leigh comes off. He will remind her of Leigh as a shoe-string would remind her of a man, and she is the kind of a woman to grow tender over a shoe-string or a foot-print, etc.

She wishes Aurora joy over the marriage she has made for her friend who loves her, and whom she loves, and whom she (Lady Waldemar) might have won if it had not been for Aurora. For this she hates Aurora as well as for the fact that in not winning the love of Romney, a possibility for virtue has been crushed out in her soul, and love become a curse instead of a heaven.

Aurora stands confounded and dazed after reading this letter, and gasps out, "Ah! not married," but Romney hastens to say that as God sees things he has a wife and child in Marian Erle and her child. Just here Marian herself appears, looking beautiful and pallid as a saint, and saying she heard Romney speaking, asks him if he means truly to take her, such as wicked men have made her, for his honorable wife ; to which he replies that he means to take her as God made her, and as men must fail to unmake her.

Marian then asks if he will take her child to be his child in the sight of men, and he declares the child shall be in every respect as his own.   She next turns to Aurora and asks her what she will say, and whether she thinks Marian will be justified in accepting this generousness of Romney's, or whether as his cousin she will object to Romney's saddling himself before the eyes of the world with a harlot wife and bastard child.   Aurora bids her accept the gift and believe that Romney is strong enough to stand up against whatever foolish worldlings might say, and she whom no breath of scandal has ever touched will clasp the hand of Marian acknowledged as pure as herself, and witness to the world that Romney is honored in his choice of Marian for his wife.

Marian smiles with a look of wonderful rapture, thanks her great Aurora, and dropping at Romney's feet, covering them with kisses, thanks God that made him so truly God-like.   When he tries to raise her, she bounds off, and standing beyond his reach tells him in impassioned words that though she is proud that he still thinks her worthy to be his wife, they two can never marry each other, for the Marian Erle that used to love him is dead ; indeed, she is not sure that she ever gave him love, because she was simply his, his slave, toy, tool, to do with as he would, that now, at any rate, she no longer loves him, but loves only her child, and that she could not bear to have any other child fathered, and with a proud race, one called happier, to vex her darling.   She hints also at the fact that there is a noble wife that Romney should wed and who loves him, meaning Aurora.

Aurora and Romney both realize at once that Marian is right.   Then Romney begs Aurora to believe he never would have spoken of his love for her that night,

knowing how she did not love him, if he had not considered himself bound to Marian, and felt that in his
utter despair he must sigh his soul out, as the most miserable wretch might choose his postures when he comes to
die. He has learned at last that he is not needed to take
care of things, since he realizes that heaven's angels will
protect Marian from the rats of society better than his
acting as her husband.

Then he swears to Aurora that though he has loved
her so deeply all these years, he would not wish things to
be any different from what they are, since he has come
to be what he is. And then he lets her know he is
blind, and that he would not have her think that he
wished her love to help the blind man stumbling.

Aurora is shocked beyond expression to learn this, and
Romney explains how in the fire Marian's father had
wounded him with a beam, and from the effects of the
hurt he became blind. When Aurora weeps for him he
seems surprised, but goes on to say that though there is
no hope for his sight there is hope for his spirit which sees
from behind the dethroned sense.

Aurora breaks down completely here and confesses at
last to Romney that she loves him, but he stops her, fearing that it is only pity for his blindness that moves her.
Aurora, however, explains that she is very vilely proud,
and though it would be easier for her to say that it was
pity had moved her love, it would not be true. She goes
on to speak of their past attitude toward each other's work,
and admits that she as well as Romney had been wrong,
in that she had not recognized the fact that love is more
than art, and that she would not be a simple woman and
own the right of love because she loves, and hearing she
is beloved is satisfied. She is changed now, she declares,
and gives herself entirely to him. After this there follows
a touching love-passage. Aurora gives some account of
what Romney said : how when a boy he had heard of the
fairy bride that was to come to him from Italy, and how
when she came he loved her from the first, and just be-

cause he loved her so much, would have her love, his highest possession, dedicated to helping him in his work for men.   But Aurora failed him, and he had taken up his work alone, and men had laughed at him.   But now they have met at last, and they will love and work together for the world, he content to do what he can among Christ's little ones, and she through the service of her art.

Line 224.   *Aftermath:* a second crop, a mowing or *math* after the first reaping.

253.   *As blue as Aaron's priestly robe:* the poet reads into the Biblical account this regret of Aaron's for his blue robes when he was stripped of his vestments at his death and they were put upon his son.   (See Numbers xx., 25, 26.)

702.   *My Cloud:* referring to the pillar of cloud by day, which preceded the Israelites through the desert. (Exodus xiii., 21.)

836-840.   *Mystic motions . . . broke in on us . . . we felt the old earth spin, And all the starry turbulence of worlds Swing round us in their audient circles:* in the claim of modern writers that a new sense of the universal being, which they call " cosmic consciousness," has come to Whitman and other seer-like souls, Elizabeth Barrett Browning should be included, upon the evidence of this passage.

845.   *The old Jewish temple's Selah-pause:* the poet's own note upon *Selah* (see " An Essay on Mind," note, line 1229, Vol. I. of this edition) quotes Calmet, who says that it is found seventy times in the Psalms, thrice in Habakkuk, and that " one conjecture is that it means the end or a pause, and that the ancient musicians put it occasionally in the margin of their psalters, to show where a musical pause was to be made and where the tune ended."

868.   *Fourier's void:* read " Fourier's dwarfed " in the first edition.

869.   *Comte:* Auguste (1798–1857), the Positivist

philosopher and friend of Fourier, both humanitarian en-
thusiasts and pioneer thinkers along lines grown familiar
to-day even if much modified.   The poet's and Aurora's
objections to their theories as well as to Romney's appear to be summed up in the preceding Book viii., lines
427-437. — *Cabet:* Étienne (1788–1856), French Com-
munist, who embodied his views in his "Voyage en
Icarie," and attempted to put them into practice in
Nauvoo on the Mississippi.

Line 885.   *Sharon gave A name to:* Song of Solomon
ii., 1.

932.   *And blow all class-walls level as Jericho's:* "So
the people shouted when the priests blew with the trum-
pets . . . with a great shout ; that the wall fell down
flat . . . and they took the city." (See Joshua vi.,
1–20.)

962-964.   *Jasper first, I said ; And second, sapphire ;
third, chalcedony; . . . last an amethyst:* alluding to
St. John's vision of the new city to be built when a new
heaven and a new earth had come to pass, as described
in Revelation xxi., 18–20.

APPENDIX.

SELECTED CRITICISM.

———

To my mind there is no poetry which equals theirs [the Brownings], which speaks so forcibly and clearly to the soul, which stirs it more deeply, in which the words are so full of meaning, which represents better the tumults and impulses of the inner being, whose influence is so powerful and keen, which lays hands on the profound and personal chords within us in order to draw forth concords so magnificent and so penetrating. In this respect it would be too long to pass their literature under review, so I will content myself with citing a recent poem — "Aurora Leigh," by Elizabeth Barrett Browning, a singular work, which is a masterpiece; indeed, I have not space to say how fine it seems to me after the twentieth perusal. It is the confession of a soul, generous, heroic, impassioned, over-full of genius; a soul whose culture has been complete; a soul philosophic and poetic, which dwells among the most elevated ideas, and yet surpasses the elevation of its ideas by the nobleness of its instincts; wholly modern by its education, by its *fierté*, by its audacity, by the constant vibration of its strained sensibility wrought to such a pitch that the least touch wakes in it an immense orchestra, and the most astonishing symphony of concords. Nothing but a soul and its intimate monologue, the sublime chant of the

great heart of young girl and of artist, drawn inwards
and struck by an enthusiasm and a pride as strong as its
own, the sustained contrast of the male and female
voices, which through the bursts and variations of the
same motive go on separating themselves and opposing
themselves more and more, until at last, suddenly
drawn together, they unite in a long, mournful, delicious duet, of a tone so exalted and so intense that there
is nothing beyond it. Formerly the epic dealt with
the foundation and destruction of cities, the combats
of the gods ; here it takes for its subject the conflicts
of ideas and passions, the changes of character ; it
takes for materials what is within instead of what is
without ; and however large may be the argument,
what is within is rich enough and great enough to fill
it. The agitations of a soul so full and so living are
equal to the clash of armies. In the absence of
legends and divine apparitions, it has its divinations of
the infinite, its dreams and its aspirations, which embrace the world ; its conceptions, stormy or luminous,
of beauty and truth ; its hell and its heaven ; its dazzling visions, ideal perspectives which open out, not
like those of Homer upon a tradition, not like those of
Dante on a dogma, but upon the summits of the most
exalted modern ideas, to gather themselves higher still
around a sanctuary and a god. There is nothing
priestly in that god ; it is that of the soul ; of a soul fer-
vent and fruitful, in which poetry becomes a religion,
which projects beyond itself its own noble instincts,
and sheds upon the nature of the infinite its own sentiment of saintly beauty. All that is expressed by a style
of a unique character, which is less a style than a musical
notation, the boldest, the most sincere, created at each
moment in such a manner that we never think of the

words ; for directly, and as it were face to face, we
see always bursting out of them the living thought ;
language strange but true to the minutest detail, alone
capable of expressing the heights and depths of the
inner life ; the accession and tumult of inspiration.

> " . . . Never flinch,
> But still, unscrupulously epic, catch,
> Upon a burning lava of a song,
> The full-veined, heaving, double-breasted age;
> That, when the next shall come, the men of that
> May touch the impress with reverent hand, and say,
> ' Behold — behold the paps we all have sucked !
> That bosom seems to beat still, or at least
> It sets ours beating.   This is living art.
> Which thus presents and thus records true life.' "

Such a style is the natural complement of such a
thought.

> " . . . Think
> Of forms less, and the external.   Trust the spirit,
> As sovran nature does, to make the form;
> For otherwise we only imprison spirit,
> And not embody.   Inward evermore
> To outward — so in life, and so in art,
> Which still is life."   . . .

Poetry thus understood has but one hero — the inner
man ; and but one style — the cry of a suffering or triumphant heart. — *Henri Taine in " Notes on England."*

AURORA . . . does not make quite an ideal
heroine.   She is either not weak enough or not strong
enough for her part in the world ; too strong to
become her cousin Romney's wife at once on his own
terms, yet not strong enough, after her spirited refusal,
either to face or silence the love and longing which for

ten years onward take the zest out of her work and the joy out of her life. And her sadness is too much in view, too long drawn out. One can imagine Lucy Snowe, or still more certainly Jane Eyre, would have taken her in hand and uttered about three pungent sentences, which, if they had not made her any happier, would all at once have taught her a great deal, cut short many plainings, and assuredly have compelled her to a demeanor of less helpless self-betrayal. For Aurora is not in the least aware how clearly she exhibits her inmost heart, not even when two or three different people have spoken out her secret before her face. At the very last, when all is set right between the two, she still says in perfect good faith :

> "'. . . As I live
> I should have died so, crushing in my hand
> This rose of love, the wasp inside and all,
> Ignoring ever to my soul and you
> Both rose and pain.'" . . .

Her self-deception on this point is more complete than the reader can quite accept as possible. No doubt the writer's difficulty is that both Aurora's and Romney's extreme dissatisfaction with themselves, and with the partial failure of their work, *have* to be exhibited in order to point the highly characteristic moral that neither devotion to poetry, nor devotion to philanthropy, is enough in itself ; both are inwardly unsatisfying and outwardly imperfect without personal love.

> " Art symbolises heaven, but Love is God
> And makes heaven." . . .

> — *Amy Sharp in " Victorian Poets."*

SHE has the vision of a great poet, but little in proportion of his plastic power. She is at home in the Universe ; she sees its laws ; she sympathizes with its motions. She has the imagination all compact — the healthy archetypal plant from which all forms may be divined, and, so far as now existent, understood. Like Milton, she sees the angelic hosts in real presence ; like Dante, she hears the spheral concords and shares the planetary motions. But she cannot, like Milton, marshal the angels so near the earth as to impart the presence other than by sympathy. He who is near her level of mind may, through the magnetic sympathy, see the angels with her. Others will feel only the grandeur and sweetness she expresses in these forms. Still less can she, like Dante, give, by a touch, the key which enables ourselves to play on the same instrument. She is singularly deficient in the power of compression. There are always far more words and verses than are needed to convey the meaning, and it is a great proof of her strength, that the thought still seems strong, when arrayed in a form so Briarean, clumsy, and many-handed.

We compare her with those great poets, though we have read her preface and see how sincerely she deprecates any such comparison, not merely because her theme is the same as theirs, but because, as we must again repeat, her field of vision and nobleness of conception are such that we cannot forbear trying her by the same high standard to see what she lacks. — *Margaret Fuller Ossoli, in " Art, Literature, and the Drama."*

. . . AURORA LEIGH . . . may . . . be pronounced a modern epic, of which the central figure is a woman, and whose theme is social amelior-

ation.   Not arms and the man, but social problems and
the woman, are sung by Mrs. Browning, and whether
she solves the problems or not, it must be admitted
that she has produced a taking and beautiful poem.   I
have always felt that it had defects, some of them
serious, but each new reading has heightened my conception of its power and splendor.   The pitch of its
intensity, sustained from beginning to end, is astonishing in a work not much shorter than " Paradise Lost."
There is no straining ; nothing to hint that the poet
worked with difficulty ; and yet the richness of ·color
and strength of imaginative fire are such as we should
look for in brief lyrical effusions rather than in a long
narrative poem.   In the rapidity and animation of the
style — the quick succession of incident, the sense of
motion everywhere — the book recalls the manner of
Homer.   It is instinct with music.   We feel that the
poet does not recite, she sings.   In its rich and ringing
melody, as well as in its warm imaginative glow, it is
superior to George Eliot's " Spanish Gypsey." . . .
The metaphoric richness, the wealth of picturesque
phrase and colored word, the animation, and even,
on the whole, the melody, of Aurora Leigh are beyond
praise.   But it lacks modulation, variety, repose.
There are, indeed, passages in which the thoughts and
images fairly float themselves away in the sphere-dance
of harmony ; wonderful passages, in which it is again
demonstrated that true melody in language is but the
rhythmic cadence natural to a mood of imaginative
thought, sufficiently elevated, calm, and mighty.   But
over wide spaces of the poem the ear finds no delight.
The crowding, the vehemence, the feverish haste and
impatience, which so frequently characterise Mr.
Kingsley's novels, can hardly fail to be recalled by

many passages. The heroine invariably talks like one
of Mr. Kingsley's characters. There is a lack of
tenderer strains to refresh and relieve the ear ; the
atmosphere wants calm, the landscape wants perspective.

But it is with the poorness of the human element
throughout the poem that I have, in the last reading,
been most painfully impressed. I am indeed not so
sure as I once was that Romney Leigh could not have
existed. He had a bee in his bonnet, but genius may
be combined with almost lunatic unpracticality. But
Marian Erle is a fancy portrait, and Lady Waldemar
is an impossibility. The only personages in the poem
whose existences are thoroughly realized are Aurora
and the aunt. Agreeable or disagreeable, Aurora has
poetic vitality. Mrs. Browning made use, without
question, of her own experiences in delineating the
successful authoress ; and though we cannot impute to
Aurora the high qualities of Mrs. Browning, or to
Mrs. Browning the flightiness and flippancy and tone
of conventional satire of her heroine, there are unmis-
takable traits of reality in the girl. The aunt, too, is
a typical English lady of a certain class, and might,
with more patient finish and more tender and intelligent sympathy, have been a lovely figure. But
Marian Erle has no life that we can call her own. She
is and does what the poet-novelist wants, neither
more nor less, exactly as a woman of wood, in an
artist's studio, wears black or white, red or green, a
widow's cap or a huntress's feather, according to the
painter's design and grouping. Lady Waldemar is not
only an extravagant caricature of aristocratic coarse-
ness in speech, but superficial and incorrect as a study
of human nature. It was most unlikely that she should
have fallen in love with such a man as Romney Leigh, yet

a woman's freakishness may account for that ; but has a clever, unprincipled, strong-willed, intriguing woman no cunning ? Could Lady Waldemar have been so childishly maladroit and indelicate as to let both Aurora and Marian into the secret of her love ? In real life such a one as Lady Waldemar would be the last person in the world to wear her heart upon her sleeve.

If the individuals described in the poem yield so little satisfaction, the classes described make no amends. Mrs. Browning fails both with the aristocracy and with the poor. We have seen her account of the reception met with by Aurora when she visited Marian Erle in St. Margaret's-court, and her description of the crowd of poor people assembled in the chapel of St. James to see Romney Leigh wed his plebeian bride. That Aurora should have been insulted in entering a house in St. Margaret's-court is of course possible ; but I think that all who have been engaged in visiting the poor in their own dwellings will admit that such an occurrence is in a high degree improbable. It cannot be said of the English poor that they are slow to recognize the wish to do them good, or to reciprocate kindly feeling. The hideous badness, the rabid ill-temper, attributed to the crowd that went from St. Giles's to see Marian Erle married to Romney Leigh prove that Mrs. Browning had no real knowledge of the London poor. Romney Leigh, a gentleman of birth and wealth, spending his money for the benefit of the destitute and miserable, and proposing to show his sense of the brotherhood of humanity by marrying a needlewoman, would have been the darling of the multitude. They would have thought him a fool, but would have loved him for all that. Instead of coming to the wedding in foul rags, they would have come in the best things they could buy, beg, or borrow. They and their babies would have been well washed at least ; their faces would have been as red as cherries or strawberries with satisfaction and jollity ; their temper would have been in a state of radiant goodness, not only on account of the delightful wedding and the expected feast, but from that appreciation of the humor of the whole affair which a London crowd would assuredly have displayed. Had such a celebration as the marriage of Romney Leigh and Marian Erle ever taken place, the appearance of the crowd would most certainly have suggested to no one that " you had stirred up hell to heave its lowest dreg-fiends uppermost." The absence of the element of humor in Mrs. Browning's mental composition is painfully conspicuous in these delineations, and is indeed fatal to their success.

So much for the class represented in this marriage on the side of Marian Erle. Now for the class represented by Romney Leigh. Aurora was placed by the bridegroom beside the altar-stair, " where he and other noble gentlemen and high-born ladies waited for the bride." Noble gentlemen and high-born ladies, the friends of Romney Leigh, ought to have been favorable representatives of the English aristocracy. . . .

Such tattle, whether uttered by aristocrats or by democrats, was surely not worthy of poetical record, and we may, I think, cherish the belief that it is impossibly vulgar and impossibly trivial. . . . Where all is improbable to the verge of pantomime, it seems idle to specify any one improbability ; but it is difficult to imagine anything more unlikely to happen than that Marian Erle should have left Romney in the lurch on the eve of her marriage. She always speaks of him with ardent enthusiasm ; his step on the stair is music to her ear ; she has no term to suit him but angel ; and yet a few glozing words from Lady Walde-mar suffice to persuade her to leave the country with-out bidding him good-by. Marian Erle would not only have been devoid of feminine ambition, pride, hope, and passion, but would have been more stupidly blind to Lady Waldemar's motives than any daughter of Eve, not a born idiot, could be, if she had per-mitted the fine lady to cheat her so easily out of a husband. Of course the pretext was that Romney would be unhappy with Marian and supremely happy with Lady Waldemar ; but she would be a strange woman who could be persuaded by a rival that the man who had chosen her must be wretched in spite of her wifely devotion to him, and that she could never be happy as his wife. . . . In the poems of Mrs. Browning are qualities which admit of their being compared with those of the greatest men ; touches which *only* the mightiest give. . . . In full recollection of Scott's vivacity, and bright, cheerful glow ; of Byron's fervid passion and magnificent de-scription ; of Wordsworth's majesty ; of Shelley's million-colored fancy ; of Coleridge's occasional flights right into the sun-glare ; of Bailey's tropic exu-berance, and of Tennyson's golden calm, I yet hold her worthy of being mentioned with any poet of this century. She has the breadth and versatility of a man ; no sameliness, no one idea, no type character ; our single Shakespearean woman. — *Peter Bayne, in " Two Great Englishwomen."*

ALTHOUGH Mrs. Browning was never at any period of her career as distinguished for finish as she was for other and more important qualities, there is yet a considerable difference in this respect between her first effusions and her later lyrics. Her strength and pathos, however, generally overwhelm all other considerations in the reader's mind, whose attention is seized and retained by personal influence. It is the poet who dares not throw himself entirely into his creations who is mostly eminent for finish. The value of the diamond to him consists in the way in which it is set, and he would prefer a stone of inferior water if it exhibited excess of polish to one much more massive if some touches of the rough still adhered to it. Yet, we are by no means contending that great poets are not also great in art. We are speaking only of finish, which is but a portion of art, and that not the most important. In art are combined the larger qualities of fitness, proportion, and truth, which are the masters of finish the world over. In all these three points Mrs. Browning was the successful artist ; and he who objected to her because he discovered here and there a false rhyme or a defective line, would have lost sight of the towering mountain ahead in stumbling over a molehill. . . .

On the work upon which, chiefly, the author's fame is conceded to rest — " Aurora Leigh " — a wide diversity of opinion exists with regard to its merits and to the position which it ought to occupy in modern literature. . . . Our own view of it is that, as a whole, it is somewhat inconsequent ; it lacks unity, for a poem of such magnitude ; but even in these higher respects, though not perfect, it is little beneath anything produced this generation. When we come to regard it in other aspects, however, our praise is almost necessarily unbounded. It is a poem which we could imagine Shakespeare dropping a tear over for its humanity. Its intense subjectivity will exempt its influence on men from decay. Were we not amazed with the beauty and fulness of its poetry, we should be struck with its philosophy. . . .

As a solution for many of the problems of social life " Aurora Leigh " must be pronounced a failure. It exhibits a wonderful sensitiveness to the evils resulting from the imperfect conditions of society, but it shows no powers of reconstruction. Its principal attraction, after its poetry, which stands supremely first therein, lies in the series of pictures of human life, in its varied phases which it presents, and in its power of analysis of the human heart. Sincerity is also a prominent characteristic of the revelations which it makes; it is an autobiography in which nothing is kept back, and the inner workings of a woman's heart were never more clearly transcribed. Unevenness characterizes the narrative, but daring speculation and rich thought are embraced within the lines. There are passages of poetry as lofty and impassioned within the covers of this one book as are contained in any single lengthy poem of which we have knowledge. From the level of occasional mediocrity we pass on to sublime imaginative heights. In this poem we have a vantage ground from which we survey the panorama of human life, illumined by the sun of genius. To attempt to extract its beauties would be futile; it is a garden in which every flower of sweetness blooms. Its aroma is amongst the most fragrant in literature. . . . A dispassionate examination of the poems of Elizabeth Barrett Browning can, we maintain, only lead to this result — that she is the equal of any poet of our time in genius. In particular qualities she may appear inferior to some who could be cited, and whose names will irresistibly suggest themselves; but in others she is as indubitably their superior; and, until we can decide who is greater, Byron or Wordsworth, Shelley or Coleridge, Homer or Shakespeare, we care not to assign her precise position. One thing is certain, however, her immortality is assured — she stands already crowned. As long as one human heart throbs for another she will be held in high esteem. Her poetry is that which refines, chastens, and elevates. We could think that with herself, as with one of her characters, "some grand blind Love came down, and groped her out, and clasped her with a kiss; she learnt God that way." And who were her teachers ? Can we ask that of one who said, " Earth's crammed with heaven, and every common bush afire with God " ? — *George Barnet Smith, in " Poets and Novelists."*

HER chiefest poem, "Aurora Leigh," might be shorter, and be the weightier for the shortness; but, as it stands, it carries more than enough of swift, true reading of human passion and purpose to stamp it as one of the richest poems of our day. . . . There are some people you can know by looking on, by talking with, by being of akin to; but there are others whom you cannot know, this way, simply because their fiery reaches of thought are too scorching for talk, and must spend themselves in poems. Mrs. Browning was spent thus. — *Geo. Wm. Curtis in Harper's Magazine, September, 1861.*

As a secondary effect of her marriage, her knowledge of the world increased; she became a keen though impulsive observer of men and women, and of the thought and action of her own time. Few social movements escaped her notice, whether in Europe or our own unrestful land ; her instincts were in favor of agitation and reform, and her imagination was ever looking forward to the Golden Year. And it was now that, summoning all her strength — alas! how unequal was her frail body to the tasks laid upon it by the aspiring soul! — with heroic determination and most persistent industry, she undertook and completed her *capo d'opera.* . . .

If Mrs. Browning's vitality had failed her before the production of "Aurora Leigh," — a poem comprising twelve thousand lines of blank verse — her generation certainly would have lost one of its representative and original creations : representative in a versatile, kaleidoscopic presentment of modern life and issues; original, because the most idiosyncratic of its author's poems. An audacious, speculative freedom pervades it, which smacks of the New World rather than the Old. Tennyson, while examining the social and intellectual phases of his era, maintains a judicial impassiveness ; Mrs. Browning, with finer dramatic insight — the result of intense human sympathy — enters into the spirit of each experiment, and for the moment puts herself in its advocate's position. "Aurora Leigh" is a mirror of contemporary life, while its learned and beautiful illustrations make it, almost, a handbook of literature and the arts. As a poem merely it is a failure, if it be fair to judge it by accepted standards. One may say of it, as of Byron's "Don Juan" (though loath to couple the two works in any comparison), that, although a most uneven production, full of ups and downs, of capricious or prosaic episodes, it nevertheless contains poetry as fine as its author has given us elsewhere, and enough spare inspiration to set up a dozen smaller poets. The flexible verse is noticeably her own, and is often handled with as much spirit as freedom; it is terser than her husband's, and, although his influence now began to grow upon her, is not in the least obscure to any cultured reader. The plan of the work is a metrical concession to the fashion of a time which has substituted the novel for the dramatic poem. Considered as a "novel in verse," it is a failure by lack of either constructive talent or experience on the author's part. Few great poets invent their myths; few prose character-painters are successful poets; the epic songsters have gone to tradition for their themes, the romantic to romance, the dramatic to history and incident. Mrs. Browning essayed to invent her whole story, and the result was an incongruous framework, covered with her thronging, suggestive ideas, her flashing poetry and metaphor, and confronting you by whichever gateway you enter with the instant presence of her very self. But either as poem or novel, how superior the whole, in beauty and intellectual power, to contemporary structures upon a similar model, which found favor with the admirers of parlor romance or the lamb's-wool sentiment of orderly British life! As a social treatise it is also a failure, since nothing definite is arrived at. Yet the poet's sense of existing wrongs is clear and exalted, and if her exposition of them is chaotic, so was the transition period in which she found herself involved. Upon the whole, I think that the chief value and interest of "Aurora Leigh" appertain to its marvellous illustrations of the development, from childhood on, of an æsthetical, imaginative nature. Nowhere in literature is the process of culture by means of study and passional experience so graphically depicted. It is the metrical and feminine complement to Thackeray's "Pendennis;" a poem that will be rightly appreciated by artists, thinkers, poets, and by them alone. Landor, for example, at once received it into favor, and also laid an unerring finger upon its weakest point. "I am reading a poem," he wrote, "full of thought and fascinating with fancy. In many pages there is the wild imagination of Shakespeare. . . . I had no idea that any one in this age was capable of such poetry. . . . There are, indeed, even here, some flies upon the surface, as there always will be upon what is sweet and strong. I know not yet what the story is. Few possess the power of construction." — *Edmund Clarence Stedman in "Victorian Poets."*

THE sins and sorrows of all that suffer wrong, the oppressions that are done under the sun, the dark days and shining deeds of the poor whom society casts out and crushes down are assuredly material for poetry of a most high order; for the heroic passion of a Victor Hugo, for the angelic passion of Mrs. Browning. — *Algernon Charles Swinburne in "Under the Microscope,"* p. 72.

No English contemporary poet by profession has left us work so full of living fire. Fire is the element in which her genius lives and breathes; . . . in moral ardor and ethical energy it [her inspiration] is unlike any other woman's, and the peculiar passion it gave to her very finest work, the rush and glow and ardor of aspiring and palpitating life, cannot properly be compared with the dominant or distinctive quality of any other poet. — *A. C. Swinburne.*